Changing Times

Changing Times

Stories of Hatfield Old and New

by Brian G Lawrence

Published October 2017

Published by Hatfield Local History Society
Printed via www.lulu.com
Copyright © 2017 – Brian G Lawrence

Based on a series of articles written by Brian G Lawrence and first published in *Hertfordshire Countryside* magazine over a period of 25 years from 1983 to 2007

All rights reserved. No part of this book may be reproduced or transmitted in any form or by any means, electronic or mechanical, including photocopying, recording, or by any information storage and retrieval system without the written permission of Brian G Lawrence.

ISBN 978-0-9928416-7-6

COVER PHOTOGRAPH

Collage of Hatfield images old and new

PREFACE

HAVING been born and brought up in a Victorian cottage that was part of Lord Salisbury's estate, it is hardly surprising that I have always felt a deep affection for Hatfield. My mother had been born in the same cottage and generations of her family had lived there ever since it was built, along with an adjoining cottage, in 1888, for the sum of £376 17s 7d. Incidentally, my father bought the cottage for the princely sum of £250 in 1950 and it remained my home for some thirty-five years.

My early schooling was at Countess Anne's Primary School in Church Street and in those days, before there was a National Curriculum, the head teacher, Miss Fielding and her staff of three ladies taught history by concentrating on local matters which cemented my interest in buildings, events and people from the surrounding area. As a young adult, I was closely involved in the cricket club where I spent hours in the company of the senior members and listened to their stories of Hatfield in earlier times as most of them had strong family connections with the town.

Even when my work took me to the South Coast, I kept in close touch with developments in the locality and this probably increased my interest in my home town. Since returning to the area and becoming a resident of St Albans for the past thirty-six years, I have strengthened my connections with my birthplace through my involvement with the Hatfield Local History Society and the Mill Green Museum. I have gained much satisfaction and knowledge through researching Hatfield's history, which continues to be one of my main interests.

Some of the developments that have taken place in Hatfield in my lifetime, particularly since it was designated one of the post-war New Towns, have not produced the benefits envisaged, however well-intentioned they were. Nevertheless, I retain the hope that this expanding community will prosper and that its residents, both present and future, will feel able to take pride in the town's glorious past.

This book reflects some of the diverse aspects of Hatfield's past that have come to my attention and interested me over many years. Hatfield has experienced major fires, Royal visits, various other noteworthy events, such as national celebrations, and major employers of labour have been attracted to the town over the years.

Residents have been fortunate to have a famous stately home and its surrounding park in their midst but it must be admitted that some of the local development that has taken place during the second half of the twentieth century has dismally failed to match their hopes and expectations.

It is my hope that this book will increase the reader's understanding of Hatfield's heritage as an enduring place of historical interest.

Brian G Lawrence

CONTENTS

Illustrations vii
Chapter 1   A Journey to School in 1942 1
Chapter 2   Hatfield Ablaze (1904 and 1908) 11
Chapter 3   Queen Victoria's Royal Visit (1846) 19
Chapter 4   King Edward VII's Royal Visit (1909) 27
Chapter 5   The Story of Hatfield Brewery 33
Chapter 6   Memories of Hatfield Park 43
Chapter 7   Hatfield's Rail Crash (1946) 51
Chapter 8   Collapse of the Wrestlers Bridge (1966) 57
Chapter 9   The Post-War Prefabs 61
Chapter 10 Hatfield's Box Factory 69
Chapter 11 Butchers Bow Out 77
Chapter 12 Looking Back – A Town That Went West . 83
Chapter 13 Looking Forward 95
Bibliography 99
Index 101

The Wrestlers Inn – first landmark on my walk to school (see Chapter 1)

Illustrations

PHOTOGRAPHS and other images, except where indicated, are from the author's private collection. Those from other sources are acknowledged in brackets, with grateful thanks.

Collage of Hatfield images old and new .... cover
The Wrestlers Inn vi
Burleigh Mead house (© Ken Wright) ix
Dagmar House with Alexandra House beyond ix
Red Lion Hotel x
Sherriff's shop and grain store x
Map of Hatfield, 1937 (Ordnance Survey) 2
Priory House, with white-painted Great Northern pub beyond 4
"Eastcott", home and surgery of Dr Leslie Burvill-Holmes 4
Looking down Brewery Hill with St Etheldreda's Church in the distance 6
View from the Broadway towards Waters Garage 6
C E Cull's, formerly Topsy's sweet shop, at end of militia cottages 8
Continuation of former militia cottages, with Jacob's Ladder on right 8
H R Taylor's barber shop with Harry Taylor in the doorway 9
Countess Anne's School at top of Church Street (© Mill Green Museum) 10
Shops in Fore Street, including Pettit's, source of a major fire in 1904 12
Hatfield's horse-drawn steam fire-engine, 1909 (© Mill Green Museum) 13
Queen Victoria entering Hatfield, 1846 (*London Illustrated News*) 18
Banquet in Marble Hall, Hatfield House, 1846 (*London Illustrated News*) 20
Queen Elizabeth's Oak, Hatfield Park 22
Stables in the Hall of the Old Palace, Hatfield Park 22
The Vineyard, Hatfield Park 22
Queen Victoria's Jubilee celebrations in Hatfield 25
Celebrating the visit of King Edward VII to Hatfield, 1909 28
More celebrations of King Edward VII's visit, near One Bell pub, 1909 28
Hatfield Brewery, c.1907 (*St James' Review*) 32
Prior Reid vehicle with some of the men 34
A later Prior Reid vehicle driven (probably) by Mr Leeke 34
Prior Reid brewery offices 40
Burnt-out brewery offices after the 1908 fire 40
Group photograph of Prior Reid employees 41

Parade at the entrance to Prior Reid brewery yard	42
Invitation to Garden Party at Hatfield House, June 19th, 1937	44
Fourth Marquess and Marchioness of Salisbury	44
Souvenir programme of "Elizabethan Pageant & Dickens Fair", 1937	46
Pageant at the "Elizabethan Pageant & Dickens Fair", 1937	46
Charity Cricket Match – teams' sheet, 1958	48
Goods train passing through Hatfield, 1958 (© Mill Green Museum)	50
Railway accident at Hatfield, 1905	55
The Wrestlers road bridge shortly after its collapse, 1966	56
Workmen dismantling the collapsed Wrestlers road bridge, 1966	56
Present-day Wrestlers footbridge (© G Philip Marris)	59
Aluminium-framed prefab erected at Birchwood after WW2	60
Children outside their prefabs	64
Children outside prefabs in Farm Way	65
Prefab at Essendon, 1998	67
Cooks Corrugated Cases Ltd, known as the "Box Factory"	70
The de Havilland Aircraft Co. Ltd	70
Jack Olding & Co. Ltd	71
Aerial view of the "Box Factory" (© Historic England archive)	74
Cooks Corrugated Cases Ltd advertisement	75
Closure of David Brewster's butcher's shop, 1998	76
T Butler & Son Ltd, family butcher's advertisement	78
Walby's butcher's shop, *c*.1900	79
H W Walby & Son advertisement	80
View of Hatfield Old Town, sometime before 1908	82
One Bell public house	84
Dray Horse public house	84
Great Northern public house – two photos	86
Great Northern public house, advertisement	88
The Galleria under construction	93
Former hangar of the de Havilland Comet airliner – now a Fitness Centre	94
Salisbury Village development building site, 2003	96
Art Deco canteen and restaurant block – now Hatfield Police Station	96
Former Hatfield Aerodrome beacon	97

Burleigh Mead house

Dagmar House with Alexandra House beyond

Red Lion Hotel

Sherriff's shop and grain store

Chapter 1   A Journey to School in 1942

MY recollections of the Great North Road in Old Hatfield date back to my early schooldays in 1942 when I walked daily from our cottage on the Great North Road—between Jack Olding's factory (now Oldings Corner Retail Park) and the Wrestlers Inn—to Countess Anne's Primary School near the Parish Church at the top of Church Street almost one-and-a-half miles away.

As I hurried past the Wrestlers, I recall it was very different from the attractive and popular hostelry of today. Then it was a rather drab little pub, subjected to the constant flow of heavy traffic negotiating the sharp bend at the nearby Wrestlers Bridge. The licensee was old Mrs Wilson, a widow, assisted by her daughter Babs. The modest amount of trade provided by the locals was supplemented by the influx of soldiers and war-workers from Jack Olding's.

After climbing the Wrestlers Hill (as we called it), the main road crossed the railway line and thereafter I would pass several substantial properties. On the left was Burleigh Mead house, the former residence of Dr Lovell Drage, while on the right were Alexandra House and Dagmar House. These had both been private schools although by this time they had ceased to be used for educational purposes. The next landmark on my journey was the Red Lion (before the Cranborne Rooms had been added), while a little further on the right-hand side of the road stood the well-kept horse trough, dated 1899. At one end of the trough there was a tap which, on a hot summer's afternoon, provided welcome refreshment on the way home from school.

Ordnance Survey Map of Hatfield, 1937

The end of my journey:
Countess Anne's School

Sherriff's shop with its large grain store on the first floor stood just beyond the trough and backed onto the railway sidings, making it ideally located for transporting its supplies. Its well-established business as corn-and-seed merchants was important both commercially and also to serve local gardeners who, at the time, were being urged to "Dig for Victory".

Continuing towards the station, I still have vivid memories of Northcotts, formerly an old family residence, which housed the Clinic. It was there that I had my first encounter with the School Dentist and the impression he made on me could be described as lasting in more ways than one. On past the Park Gates and the Station yard to the Great Northern pub at the top of Arm and Sword Yard. Standing on the opposite corner of the Yard was another substantial building, Priory House, occupied by the Gas Board. This I remember for its highly polished brown linoleum which squeaked beneath the shoes of this small schoolboy as he was led into the Offices to pay the quarterly bill.

The next buildings on the left were the library and the Public Hall, while opposite, alongside the alley leading to the footbridge, was the imposing house of the family doctor, Leslie Burvill-Holmes. The waiting-room for his patients was bare, a rather dark room which one entered from the alley by the footbridge. A visit to the doctor usually entailed a fairly long wait on hard wooden benches since he was not only a sole practitioner but, for many years, a local councillor as well, and thus his surgery times were very approximate. In the fullness of time, the surgery door would suddenly swing open, operated automatically by the doctor by means of a series of cords and pulleys from behind his untidy desk.

A friendly greeting and sympathetic ear would quickly make the patient feel better, and the presence of one of his well-behaved bull terriers would add to the homeliness of the surroundings.

A row of shops led from the Public Hall down Brewery Hill, as it was known to the locals, although I did not appreciate the origin of the name since the Brewery had long since closed.

Priory House, with white-painted Great Northern pub beyond

"Eastcott", home and surgery of Dr Leslie Burvill-Holmes. Alleyway on far left led to footbridge over the railway line to Beaconsfield Road.

The first of the shops was Drury's, the gentlemen's outfitters run by the cheerful, rotund Mr Nott, who travelled daily from Hertford. Then came Charlie Taylor's sweet shop, Dollimore's the greengrocer and Mervyn Powell the photographer who was called in to record all noteworthy local events. Hollier's Dairy Shop, with a china cow in the window, stood prominently on the bend of the hill. Hill & Simmons the baker's and Butlers the butcher's completed the row of shops leading to Waters Garage with its petrol pumps placed at random in front.

Down the hill on the right-hand-side of the road, the shops were more modern in appearance and these buildings still stand today in what is now Salisbury Square. First there was Dewhurst the butcher's, and then the International Stores, probably the largest single shop in the old town. It was here that my mother registered for her grocery rations, so I got to know this shop and the staff quite well, in particular Mr Jennings, the manager, who stood at the far end of the shop, Mr Flegg on the groceries and Nobby Clark, who mounted guard over the bacon-slicer. It was not until some thirteen years later that I entered the next building, the offices of the Westminster Bank, when I called there one day in 1955 to see the Manager, seeking employment.

The next shop was McSweeney's the chemist's—so up-to-date in its lay-out and contrasting sharply with the only other chemist's shop in the old town. The latter, run by Mr Cox in Fore Street, still had a very Dickensian appearance about it and was distinctive in that you entered by going down a step from the pavement. As the door opened and the bell rang, a white-haired old man shuffled forward from the back of the shop, feebly whistling, having reluctantly suspended the mixing of some obscure potion made to a time-honoured prescription.

Returning to the Great North Road, after the chemist's shop one passed the butcher's shop belonging to Joe Walby, which would continue to trade for a further fifty years, though under different ownership.

Looking down Brewery Hill with St Etheldreda's Church in the distance.
On the near left is Butler's the butchers with Waters Garage beyond.

View from the Broadway back towards Waters Garage.
Around the bend led back to the railway station.

The last of the shops in this block to be occupied at that time was a ladies' hairdresser's, "Julie's" by name, I believe, although you will appreciate that a shop of that description was of very little interest to a small boy of five.

At the bottom of Brewery Hill, the Great North Road was known as the Broadway—not particularly broad, but lined with lime trees on each side. I recall on the right-hand side of the road a small café which stood in front of the Catholic Church, a large unoccupied shop which I believe had previously been part of the Waters Garage enterprise and at one time a branch of the Welwyn Department Store. The final shop on this side of the road was a small shoe repairer's owned by Mr Elliott on the corner of Batterdale. On the other side, between the yards of the One Bell and Dray Horse public houses, was a shoe shop run by the Worrall Brothers, who later moved to the larger vacant premises opposite.

My walk along the Great North Road ended at the Salisbury Hotel, and my recollections beyond that point—along what was known as the London Road—are hazy, though I was on occasions reluctantly dragged into Mrs Richardson's wool shop. The only shop of importance to me and my five-year-old school friends was Topsy's sweet shop at the end of Salisbury Square, which we could invade easily after school via Jacob's Ladder. In one of the old militia cottages opposite the Salisbury Hotel lived Ben Bishop, a veterinary surgeon of undisclosed qualifications who, on being summoned, would arrive on an ancient bicycle to advise on the treatment of one of our family pets.

After turning the corner between the Dray Horse and Salisbury Hotel, my route allowed me to glance into the large windows of Daisy Gray's toy shop, a veritable Aladdin's Cave, where most of my pocket money was spent on lead soldiers and, later, my early Dinky Toys. As I turned into Church Street for the final haul up to school, I passed the barber's shop where Harry Taylor, assisted by his wife, would patiently cut the hair of the army of protesting small boys who were dragged into the shop by their mothers to be smartened up after school.

C E Cull's (formerly Topsy's sweet shop) at end of former Militia Cottages. The shop faced onto what was then the Great North Road.

Continuation of the former Militia Cottages, with Jacob's Ladder on the right, leading to Church Street

Taylor's barber shop with Harry Taylor (left) in the doorway

Occasionally, my return journey would be varied to satisfy my mother's shopping needs. Perhaps we would go down Batterdale—Pond Hill to the older generation—past Lawson's hardware shop to Jim Smith's the fishmonger, which was opposite the Fire Station. Jim Smith was later to move to a smart new shop on the Great North Road between the International Stores and the Westminster Bank, in premises subsequently incorporated into the Bank. This move shortened his daily trip to the railway station with his trolley to collect the fresh fish.

My other possible detour would be along the side of Daisy Gray's to the bottom of Fore Street to call in at Steabben's the butcher's—next to the Eight Bells pub—or at one of the two Hankins shops, the drapery store at the corner of Park Street or the gentlemen's outfitters in Fore Street, where Stan Hankin himself could usually be found.

To a small wide-eyed boy, all these landmarks had every appearance of permanence, which Hitler and all the austerity of the Second World War could do little to disrupt. In less than twenty years, however, only the relics of this part of Old Hatfield would still be standing after the planners had set their minds to work.

Journey's End: Countess Anne's School (at the top of Church Street)

Chapter 2   Hatfield Ablaze (1904 and 1908)

THE most widely reported fire tragedy in Hatfield's history was that which took place on the evening of 22 November 1835, destroying the West Wing of Hatfield House and killing the dowager Marchioness of Salisbury. However, in the first decade of the twentieth century, two major conflagrations broke out in the heart of Hatfield which caused mayhem at the time and might easily have changed the face of the old town as we know it today.

Many visitors to the town remember Fore Street as its most attractive street with its mixture of architecture and quaint houses—a quiet backwater leading to the Parish Church and to Hatfield Park. Events that took place on an autumn night in 1904 could have destroyed all that and led to a disaster even greater than that which beset the old town when the developers moved in during the 1960s.

On the evening of Tuesday 11 October 1904, a young lad by the name of Harry Winter, employed by Messrs Pettit & Co., the grocery and general stores in Fore Street, was sent to get oil from a store alongside the stables behind the shop. As it was dark, the lad struck a match and its burnt end dropped onto some spilt oil. The alarm was raised immediately and the local fire brigade, under the direction of Captain Tom Christian, quickly arrived on the scene. Unfortunately, the fire engine was defective and it was not easy to get to the source of the fire which was between the buildings in Fore Street and those in Church Street (then known as Back Street).

Despite these difficulties, the firemen soon got their hoses to work from both directions, gaining access through the premises of Messrs Payne, the saddler's next door to Pettit's shop.

Looking up Fore Street from the junction with Park Street. Pettit's shop (source of the blaze) is up the hill just beyond the narrow white building

The fire brigade from Hatfield House arrived to provide valuable assistance but, by this time, the buildings at the rear of several of the Fore Street shops were enveloped in flames. The store-houses behind the shops contained gunpowder and benzole. Inevitably there was a series of explosions as the fire reached these inflammable materials, shattering windows throughout the town and sending the onlookers running for their lives as they tried to avoid the flying debris. The danger of further explosions persisted as Captain Christian and his men concentrated their efforts on the main source of the fire. After about an hour, it was brought under control but not before considerable damage had been done to the buildings at the rear of Messrs Pettit's shop and the adjoining premises. In fact, the fire brigade had to continue their work until at least 10 p.m. and, fortunately, there was still a small team on duty to deal with a minor outbreak as the flames burst out again around midnight.

Hatfield's horse-drawn double vertical steam engine purchased in 1909 from Shand Mason & Co. It cost £310, had a pumping capacity of 300 gallons per minute and could discharge a jet to the height of 150 feet.

In these modern days of instant communication, it is difficult for us to imagine the confusion that such an event would cause, but eye-witness reports demonstrated the impact in neighbouring towns. As the St Albans fire brigade "galloped through the town" to respond to the call for assistance, rumours circulated among the citizens that Hatfield House was on fire. Cyclists and pedestrians streamed along the Hatfield Road to see the conflagration and spread their stories of the impending disaster at the home of the Cecils.

With the flames rising higher than the roofs of the buildings, the residents of both Fore Street and Church Street were gathering together their furniture and other possessions fearing that the fire would spread to their homes. The stables at the rear of the Fore Street shops were the cause of great concern once the firemen were satisfied that human life was no longer in danger.

Eventually, men reached the animals which had to be blindfolded with sacks before they could be exposed to the heat and flames. Six horses and a heifer cow were led to safety in this way by the rescuers. By the time the fire engines from St Albans and Hertford arrived, the local brigade, with support from the Hatfield House brigade, had brought the main blaze under control and averted a major disaster.

Lord Salisbury and other members of his family, including his brother the Rector, were conspicuous at the scene, providing comfort and assistance to the residents in any way they could. It should not be overlooked that although Fore Street had by that time ceased to be part of the main route from London to the North, it was still very much the major shopping centre of the town and the hub of the community.

The firm of Pettit & Co., where the fire broke out, was undoubtedly an important store in those days as may be seen from the following feature article which appeared in *The St James' Review* a few years later in 1907. It read:

> It is a feature in the conduct of business by Messrs Pettit & Co., that nothing is sold the purity of which cannot be guaranteed. They cut only the best bacon, the butter and lard are only kept in quantities that can be depended upon; the jams, pickles, condiments and preserves are by manufacturers of responsibility—Lazenby, Chivers, Crosse and Blackwell. And so also the innumerable potted and canned goods: meat, soups, game, fruit and vegetables; *hors d'oeuvres* for the breakfast and luncheon table—articles of which the merest suspicion of inferior quality should not be entertained.
>
> At the back of the premises in Fore Street is a large building of two floors, built in 1881, and used as a general store. Here we come upon stocks of every conceivable gardening utensil, also garden sand, galvanised iron sheets, barbed and other wire, tar felting, and so on. In another part are stored various foods for domestic and sporting dogs, poultry mixtures, and molassine meal. Then again, oils and tallow-chandlery, and various painters' sundries. Elsewhere we meet with turnery and hardware, and reserve stocks of sugar, rice, bags and string. In 1905 a new coach-lodge was erected, with stabling, and over this a hay-loft, provided with a hoist and entrance from the back street.

> Nor does this exhaust the available space, for there are two cellars under the shop that are utilised for storage.
>
> The range of articles supplied is very comprehensive, and as supplemental to the goods already enumerated, we would say that Messrs Pettit have the agency in Hatfield for Mazawattee Tea, that they are large dealers in cigars, and stock the principal proprietary brands of cigarettes and packet tobaccos. Cutlery, electro-plate, clocks, pocket knives, etc., all come within their sphere of activity and command attention at the hands of a wide circle of patrons.

By the time this article was written, the firm was trading from 15 and 17 Fore Street, having apparently taken over the premises formerly occupied by Francis Dunham the builder. The reference to a new coach-lodge erected in 1905 suggests that this was financed from the insurance claim made on their Atlas Fire Policy. So, all in all, the business suffered no long-term adverse effects from the careless action of one of its employees and, in fact, the firm continued to flourish until the early 1930s. One can but wonder what the outcome was for the poor unfortunate Harry Winter.

Comments made after the fire led Captain Christian to write to the Parish Council requesting additional modern equipment to enable the town's fire brigade to deal with any future outbreaks. He pointed out that their existing leather hosepipe was over twenty-years old and he sought lengths of canvas hose with instantaneous couplings, two stand pipes, two branch pipes, two interchangeable couplings and breaching. He emphasised the disadvantages they suffered as a result of not being equipped with ladders and requested the provision of two ladders of twenty-five and thirty-five rounds. His *cri de coeur* received a favourable response from the Council and the request was granted with three stand-pipes being provided rather than the two requested.

The demands made by Captain Christian illustrate very clearly the magnitude of the task they faced on that October evening with only very basic equipment at their disposal. In the circumstances, the gratitude extended by the townsfolk to the men who fought the blaze was thoroughly deserved as their prompt action had surely averted a catastrophe in the heart of the town.

Some three-and-a-half years after the Fore Street fire, the men of the Hatfield Fire Brigade were once more put to the test when, in the early hours of Sunday 24 May 1908, fire broke out in part of Pryor, Reid & Co.'s Brewery. Fortunately there was no loss of life but there was extensive damage, particularly to the building that housed the brewery offices and the mineral-water manufacturing plant, which was completely gutted.

The dramatic account of the disaster tells how Mr Eaton, an employee of the brewery who lived on the premises, was aroused by his Irish Terrier, Mick, shortly before 3 a.m. He immediately ran to the home of Captain Christian who, in addition to being the Captain of the Fire Brigade, was also the brewery manager. A call-boy was despatched to gather up the team of firemen and a telephone call was made to the St Albans Fire Brigade.

Fortunately, Captain Christian was in the unique position of having an intimate knowledge of the premises and he and his team, ably supported once more by the Hatfield House brigade commanded by Mr J Pateman, quickly set to work. Using water from Carter's Pond near the South Front of Hatfield House, and doubtlessly benefiting from their new equipment, the team was able to fight the flames with "a grand supply of water at high pressure".

Captain Christian took responsibility for entering the blazing building to rescue as many of the firm's books and other valuable records as possible. He was only too well aware that the seat of the fire in the building known as New Place contained large quantities of sugar and syrup and incorporated the carpenter's workshop where the packing cases were constructed. If the fire had reached this part of the building, there was only a lath-and-plaster wall separating it from the china and glassware shop on the corner of Park Street which was the home of the Gregory family.

The Captain's detailed knowledge, coupled with the fearless efforts of the Hatfield and St Albans firefighters, managed to contain the fire within the brewery premises. Although the old building was wrecked and much of the equipment reduced to a pile of twisted ironwork, charred wood and rubble, the firemen, equipped with the additional superior engine from St Albans—capable of directing a significantly greater volume of water on to the flames—completed their task by 7.30 a.m. Eyewitnesses told of residents from nearby properties all pouring out onto the street in their nightclothes and doing what they could to assist the shopkeepers in Park Street whose premises were in immediate danger. Those particularly threatened were Gregory's which adjoined the brewery premises, Hankin's the draper's and Jessop's the baker's which were all frantically engaged in moving furniture, stocks and other valuables into Chapman's Yard or into buildings further from the fire in Fore Street.

Everyone was full of admiration for the splendid work of all the firefighters but special praise was extended to Captain Christian who had displayed remarkable energy and endurance for a man of seventy-two years of age. Many of the onlookers were most impressed by the equipment which had been brought by the St Albans Fire Brigade, especially the fire engine, which the majority of the locals had probably never seen before. Realising how vital it had been in containing the fire and preventing the loss of life, the Hatfield residents immediately took up the call that their "first-class brigade of men" must be provided with "a steamer with the least possible delay".

The extent of the damage to the brewery premises was estimated in the region of £5–6,000 but, whilst the building was fully covered, the machinery was not insured up to anything like its full value. Nevertheless, indications are that the rebuilding work got underway with no great delay and the business continued to prosper for a further decade. In fact, the brewery received an unexpected royal visit shortly after the fire on the morning of Tuesday 13 October 1908, as the King's car, taking him to Newmarket races, burst a tyre on approaching Hatfield. Reports of the incident state that, whilst the chauffeur was changing the wheel, His Majesty strolled into the brewery yard, sat down on a barrel and watched with interest the work of reconstructing the mineral-water factory.

Queen Victoria entering the town of Hatfield (1846)

Chapter 3   Queen Victoria's Royal Visit (1846)

THE Royal party left Cassiobury, Watford, immediately after lunch at about 3 p.m. on Thursday 22 October 1846, escorted by a detachment of the Herts Yeomanry. About four miles from Hatfield, they were met by Lord Salisbury, the Duke of Wellington, Lord Charles Wellesley, Lord Robert Cecil and Mr J M Balfour on horseback. Once the Queen had greeted her escort, the cortège proceeded to Hatfield arriving in the town at 4.15 p.m.

At Hatfield, the preparations were "picturesque and in appropriate taste". The display commenced at Puttock's Oak (at the top end of Beaconsfield Road) where a triumphal arch of laurel, studded with fuchsias, had been erected. At the junction of the Great North Road and St Albans Road, a "body of tenantry of the Marquis of Salisbury" wearing blue rosettes joined the procession. Facing the house of Dr Thomas was a pretty arch of evergreens and garlands of flowers, flanked with Union Jacks, and surmounted with a smaller flag. On the arch, the letters VR were inscribed in dahlias, and were also inscribed in the illumination lamps at Dr Thomas's residence. At the foot of the hill (Fore Street), another evergreen arch, surmounted with a Royal Crown and flags, had been erected. As the Royal procession approached, the Welwyn band played "God Save the Queen". The scene along Fore Street was truly exhilarating, with crowds lining the street and with flags and evergreens decorating every house.

The visit took place some years before the Great North Road was diverted away from Hatfield Park and Fore Street. After it passed St Etheldreda's Parish Church, where there was another decorated

The Banquet in the Marble Hall, Hatfield House (1846)

arch, the procession turned right along the London Road to approach Hatfield House from the South Front.

The Marquess of Salisbury, having conducted Her Majesty into the Park, then "galloped up the avenue" in sufficient time to receive his guests on their arrival. Two companies of the South Herts Yeomanry, with band and colours, formed a guard of honour in the courtyard. Having been greeted by members of Lord Salisbury's family, the Royal visitors were escorted to the King James Room where the Duke of Wellington and other guests, including the Marquess and Marchioness of Exeter, Earl and Countess Spencer, Earl and Countess Brownlow, Lord Sandys, Lord and Lady Braybrooke, and Lord and Lady Charles Wellesley, awaited them.

In the evening, a lavish banquet took place in the Marble Hall. The table was decorated with gold candelabra and vases of flowers. Chinese lanterns were suspended from the ceiling. The attendants were in full dress and each wore a silver badge of the Salisbury arms on the left coat-sleeve. At the end of the meal, the Marquess of Salisbury proposed the loyal toast and a military band in the gallery played the National Anthem. After a further toast to Prince Albert, the band played the "Coburg March".

The ladies then retired to the King James Room to be followed shortly afterwards by Prince Albert, the host and the other male guests. The evening's entertainment concluded with the appearance of twelve German artists singing a collection of popular German airs.

On the following morning, the Park—and in particular the court on the North Front—was a hive of activity with the traditional roasting of a whole bullock. For most of the House guests, Friday began with a service in the Chapel, though it appears that the Queen and Prince Albert did not attend. After breakfast, the Prince accompanied by Lord Salisbury and several others went out shooting. It is recorded that the Prince killed 140 head out of a total kill of 158 pheasants, 4 hares, 150 rabbits and 4 partridges.

Queen Elizabeth's Oak

Stables in Hall of the Old Palace

The Vineyard

After lunch, Prince Albert drove Her Majesty in a pony-drawn phaeton carriage through the Park where they were greeted warmly by the townsfolk. They made their first stop at Queen Elizabeth's Oak, the trunk of which by that time had been protected by a lead-covering and was enclosed by a low fence. The Queen was given a small branch lopped from the tree. The party then drove on, preceded by their host on horseback, to the "curious garden" known as the Vineyard, where they enjoyed the tranquil scene of secluded walks and the gentle River Lea. Before returning to the House, the party stopped off to admire the remains of the Old Palace which was then in use as stables for thirty-two horses.

Meanwhile, activity on the North Front of Hatfield House reached fever-pitch as the iron cradle in which the ox had been roasted was moved onto a truck drawn by several locals ("rustics") to the tables as some two-to-three-thousand townsfolk looked on, offering noisy encouragement. The tables were laid for four-to-five-hundred and they sat down to a feast of ample portions of beef with "hunches" of bread and an inexhaustible supply of ale from the row of barrels that had been lined up for the occasion. The meal was consumed "with high relish" and the scene was watched by a party from the House, including the Prime Minister who had come down to "witness this rude rustic banquet".

Dinner for the Royal party and their guests was followed by a lavish Ball held in the Grand Gallery. Those invited to the Ball began to arrive from 9 p.m. but it was not until 10.30 p.m. that the Queen, accompanied by her host, arrived in the Gallery where a "temporary throne" had been set up for her Majesty. Once the formalities had been completed, the Ball opened with a quadrille in which the Queen danced with her host. After some two hours of festivities, the Royal party, followed by the other guests, proceeded to the Marble Hall where supper was served, before the company dispersed with the last carriages leaving by 2 a.m. The event was, not surprisingly, depicted as a joyous occasion but later accounts, such as that given by Lord David Cecil in his book *The Cecils of*

Hatfield House, paint a rather different picture. Referring to the Royal guests, he wrote:

> Neither ... made a good impression on the company. The Prince Consort smiled at nobody; instead, he stared restlessly about, now and again fixing his eyes on someone and then whispering about that person to the Queen. She was more affable; but she joined in the whispering and looked unbecomingly fat.

Despite the inclement weather on the Saturday morning, the Prince joined the shooting party, credited with killing a further 300 head of game. The Queen passed the morning viewing some of the treasures in the Library and other parts of the House. The Queen and Prince Albert concluded their visit by planting two oak saplings in the East garden. Just before 3 p.m. the Royal carriages departed in heavy rain amid loud cheers from the assembled crowd.

Lord Salisbury on horseback accompanied her Majesty as far as St Albans. The procession, with military escort, continued through Watford, Moor Park, Pinner, Harefield and Uxbridge arriving at Windsor Castle at about six o'clock. It was observed that "her Majesty and the Prince looked extremely well and in excellent spirits after their journey".

Whatever the true feelings of the Royal visitors about the visit may have been, the indications are that Lord Salisbury, their host, viewed it with great satisfaction for, in the following year, he commanded the building of a shingled spire on the Parish Church to commemorate the Queen's visit. The spire remained a dominant feature on the Hatfield skyline until it was taken down in 1930.

Looking back over more than 170 years, it is not easy for us to envisage the impact the private Royal visit would have had on the mass of the population of the town. To put it into perspective, we must try to understand the social conditions that existed for most people with their humdrum lives of toil and with only extremely rare distractions from the weekly routine. It was a constant struggle to get sufficient food and clothing for the family, and with little prospect of any real change in conditions for the better during their lifetimes.

Queen Victoria's Jubilee celebrations in Hatfield.

Another glimpse of nineteenth-century life for the masses some forty years later can be obtained from a report on the celebrations that took place in Hatfield, just as in every other town in the land, for Queen Victoria's Golden Jubilee in June 1887.

It was a beautifully fine day and the town was tastefully decorated with flags, mottoes and evergreens. Special mention was made of Mr Groom's house (probably in Fore Street) which bore the motto "We hail the Jubilee of our Queen; God Bless Her."

Throughout the morning, groups of locals in holiday mood gathered round the town. At noon, a service was held in the Parish Church. When the service was over, groups began to wend their way through Hatfield Park into the Riding School which was attractively decorated with wreaths and flags. At 2 p.m. the building was filled with about 650 of the poor of the town seated at the fourteen tables which had been laid out for their feast. No details are given of the meal itself but the report stresses that they "did full justice to the good things provided". This was hardly surprising as the menu probably included more meat and nourishing food than many of those seated in the Riding School that day would enjoy from one year to the next. The meal was preceded by, and ended with, the singing of "God Save the Queen" followed by an address by the rector, the Rev. W C Talbot.

The rest of the afternoon was given over to a long programme of sports, although I suspect that many of the diners were by then lying in the shade of the trees sleeping off the effects of their feast.

At 5.30 p.m. about 1,200 children and others sat down to tea after which the sports continued until 9 p.m. As dusk fell, "God Save the Queen" again rang out and the crowds began to disperse, "all delighted with the day's enjoyment".

Accounts of Hatfield after dark on that festive night concentrate on the attractive decorations that could be seen in every window of the gas and lantern-lit houses. No mention is made of unruly behaviour though it is unimaginable that, after such high-spirited celebrations, it was all calm and trouble-free in and around the host of beer houses and inns that were a feature of Park Street, Arm and Sword Yard, Fore Street and other parts of the town. Let us assume that the goodwill engendered throughout the day left behind a measure of tolerance and understanding that would be sustained on that memorable night.

Such an occasion would have been deeply engraved in the memories of all those present and would surely have been recounted by them in vivid detail to later generations of their families for years to come.

Based on accounts published in "Illustrated London News" on 24 and 31 October 1846 and "Herts Advertiser" on 25 June 1887.

Chapter 4   King Edward VII's Royal Visit (1909)

NOWADAYS, members of the Royal Family know that any visit they make is likely be covered by television cameras and photographers, both authorised and on many occasions unauthorised, with pictures and reports flashed across the world almost instantaneously. How different it was before this sophisticated technology became so readily available, when Royalty and other prominent figures of the day were surrounded in mystique and were much more remote from the main bulk of the population.

With this in mind, it is interesting to look back at the visit of the King and Queen to Hatfield in 1909. King Edward VII was no stranger to the town and, in the early days of the twentieth century, the local press referred to at least two occasions when he made unofficial stops in Hatfield. The first was on Tuesday 23 October 1906 when he ordered his driver to stop the car near the station to enable him to view the statue to the Third Marquess of Salisbury which had been unveiled in a ceremony just three days earlier. The King is also reported to have strolled through the streets of the town and into the brewery yard on the morning of Tuesday 13 October 1908 when a burst tyre led to his being delayed as he was being driven to Newmarket races.

The visit of the King and Queen on Saturday 12 June 1909 was a much more organised affair. Although planned as a private visit to spend the weekend with the Marquess and Marchioness of Salisbury, the townsfolk were keen to play a full part in providing a warm welcome to the Monarch. A committee, which had been hastily formed just a few days before the visit, made it their priority

Celebrating the visit of King Edward VII in the Great North Road

More celebrations near the One Bell pub

to ensure that the heart of the town was appropriately decorated. Elaborate decorations consisting of a series of Venetian poles wreathed in evergreen foliage, rhododendrons and streamers of pendant flags were erected along both sides of the Great North Road from the old London Road School at the south end of the town (near the present roundabout at the junction with French Horn Lane) to the railway station and throughout the length of Fore Street. Triumphal arches were located outside the school, at the main entrance to the Park and at the bottom of Fore Street. The first of the decorated arches bore the message "Hatfield welcomes our beloved King and Queen", the second "God save the King" and the third "God bless their Majesties". Fore Street, in particular, was a blaze of colour with scarcely a house lacking a flag or similar decoration.

Early on the Saturday afternoon, crowds from Hatfield and the surrounding district began to line the route through the town and in the Park. Spectators were allowed as far as the quadrangle at the North Front of Hatfield House but the eighty policemen on duty, including six mounted officers, experienced no problems in controlling a good-natured and orderly crowd.

The Royal party was expected to arrive from Buckingham Palace at about 4.30 p.m. but it was not until an hour later that the vehicles appeared, greeted by "lusty cheers from the crowd" and, as the Royal visitors went past, "nearly every man doffed his hat".

The cars drove through the Park to the South Front of the House where their Majesties received the Royal salute from the bodyguard formed by a hundred members of the Herts Battalion of Infantry drawn from St Albans, Hertford and Hatfield and the Regimental Band played the National Anthem. Lord and Lady Salisbury received their Royal guests after which the King inspected the bodyguard before they marched off. Once the formalities had been completed, the party adjourned to the King James Drawing Room for tea and, to round off the day, dinner was served in the Marble Hall.

Sunday's brilliant weather drew large crowds to Hatfield in the hope of seeing the Royal visitors who were expected to attend the Parish Church. However, plans were changed and it was decided to hold Matins in the private chapel in Hatfield House where the Rev. Lord William Cecil officiated.

Later in the morning, Lord and Lady Salisbury accompanied by their Majesties and other members of the house party strolled down to the Parish Church but, by that time, the morning service was over and the disappointed crowd had dispersed. The King was particularly struck with the Salisbury Chapel and showed great interest in the tablet marking the burial place of Lord Melbourne—though press reports incorrectly referred to Palmerston.

It was noted that the ladies in the party were without hats and that the Queen had her toy spaniels with her. From the Church, the party moved on to the tomb of the late Marquess of Salisbury which they viewed for some minutes in "silent contemplation". They then stopped off at the Old Palace which was in use as stables. Inside, the King displayed particular interest in the "fine old roof" as he strolled up and down puffing a cigar. Throughout the Royal "walk about", Princess Victoria was eagerly taking photographs with her little hand camera—no doubt quite a novelty at that time.

Undeterred by the change of plan that prevented many from catching a glimpse of the visitors earlier in the day, another large crowd gathered in the afternoon both inside the Park and along the streets. This time, they were rewarded by seeing their Majesties and the other guests leaving by car for a visit to Knebworth Hall.

Before departing for Windsor on Monday morning, the King and Queen performed a final ceremony by each planting a cedar tree in the gardens on the South West side of Hatfield House. There are still cedar trees growing in that part of the grounds which, according to their size, could be those planted by the King and Queen. But since they are not designated in any way, this cannot be confirmed.

Early on the Monday morning, in preparation for the Royal departure, the townsfolk had been busy "freshening up" the decorations by removing any withered foliage and replacing it with freshly cut flowers and plants. They must have felt their efforts had been worthwhile when the Royal cars passed through the Old Palace gateway and drove down Fore Street at a walking pace. The King, dressed in a light grey suit, bowler hat and goggles, travelled in an open car and repeatedly acknowledged the hearty cheers of the local residents. The route westwards took the party through Hatfield "Newtown" where their Majesties were given another greeting as they sped through.

After the weekend celebrations, the town was still in carnival mood on the Monday evening. At short notice, the place had been illuminated with torches and Chinese lanterns and, at 9 p.m., a procession marched through the streets, up to Newtown and then back into the Park. The procession included clowns, *Pierrots*, the Boys' Brigade, drill classes, the fire brigade's "awkward squad" under "General" Sharp, "Britannia", her attendants and a host of other characters.

There followed a couple of hours of "general frolic" with dancing to the strains of the Welham Green Band and a display of fireworks. The festivities culminated with an address from Lord Salisbury at Hatfield House where he thanked the people for their assistance in making the Royal visit such a success. The gathering dispersed at about midnight after the singing of the National Anthem and "Auld Lang Syne".

Hatfield Brewery, c.1907

Chapter 5   **The Story of Hatfield Brewery**

MY earliest recollections of Hatfield do not go back to the days when the brewery flourished, although older residents still referred to a stretch of the Great North Road in Old Hatfield as Brewery Hill. The name Pryor Reid, the last owners of the brewery, was still quite fresh in their memories.

In common with so many other small towns, the business of brewing and malting had been carried on in Hatfield for hundreds of years. Records show the Searancke family to be the earliest to be associated with brewing in the locality. Of Flemish origin, the family can be traced back to Essendon in 1545 and they are also credited with introducing hops into Hertfordshire. Members of the family are known to have been farming and brewing in the nearby villages of Woodside and Wildhill during the sixteenth and seventeenth centuries and John Searancke is known to have come to Hatfield by 1582 and to have been the owner of a small brewery behind the Chequers Inn at the bottom of Fore Street by 1610.

After the death of John Searancke in 1617, several generations of the family continued the brewery business in the town. Throughout the seventeenth century and for much of the eighteenth century, the family and brewery prospered. The last of the direct male descendants to run the brewery, also called John Searancke, was undoubtedly a man of considerable stature and influence in the locality, being not only a successful businessman but also a Justice of the Peace as well as Deputy Lieutenant and High Sheriff of the County. At the time of his death in 1779, he owned a considerable amount of property including 1,000 acres in Philadelphia, USA.

Pryor Reid vehicle with some of the men

A later vehicle with driver (probably) Mr Leeke and Joe Hornet alongside

As John Searancke died childless, his will decreed that the property be left to his three sisters. But within ten years (in 1789), ownership had passed to his nephew Francis Carter Searancke, son of one of the sisters who had inherited the business in 1779. This raises the question as to why the owner should still be called Searancke. It is believed that he had, in fact, changed his name from Niccoll in 1781 to comply with the terms of his uncle's will.

Francis Searancke also had other brewing interests in St Albans at Kingsbury Brewery which he had acquired in 1782 on the death of his father, Francis Carter Niccoll, a former Mayor of St Albans. In 1815, Searancke decided to devote his full attention to the St Albans business and thus he sold his interest in the Hatfield Brewery to Joseph Bigg, who had been his business partner for several years, for £11,154.

The next few years must have seen the Hatfield Brewery pass through difficult times since, by 1819, Bigg had become bankrupt and the brewery with his other property was acquired by Joseph Field for £19,500. He carried out various improvements to the business and saw it on the road to recovery by the time of his death in 1836. The record of the sale following his death gives a good indication of the size of the business at that time. It referred to "that old-established and respectable concern, the Hatfield Brewery said to own forty licensed houses in Hatfield, Herts, Beds, Middlesex and Essex, and producing upward of 7,600 barrels annually".

The business was purchased at auction, held at the Red Lion, by James Spurrell, brother-in-law of James Watney, for £24,350. However, within a few months, he had sold the brewery to the Pryor family, which leads us to the final chapter of this story.

The Pryors were originally an East Anglian family whose association with Hertfordshire dates back to the fourteenth century when Thomas Priour [*sic*] was granted land at Baldock by King Edward III. Thereafter, nothing can be traced of the family for some 300 years but we are able to pick up their story again during the seventeenth century. It was at that time that, as Quakers, they came into conflict with the authorities—there are several references to members of the Pryor family spending time in Hertford gaol. Towards the end of the century, with the passing of the Toleration Act, persecution came to an end and the Pryors, in common with many other Quaker families, began to enjoy a period of greater prosperity.

It was Robert Pryor who built up a substantial malting business in Baldock and this was passed on to his eldest son John on his death in 1744. During the second half of the eighteenth century, John Pryor became a well-known and respected brewer and maltster in the town and, in addition, farmed his own land, including that which he inherited from his mother's brother, John Izzard. By the time of his death in 1819 his estate was substantial and, under the terms of his will, it was divided among his six children (four sons and two daughters).

The eldest son, John Izzard Pryor, took over the brewery whilst the youngest son, Vickris, acquired the maltster's business. It is interesting to record that the other two sons, Thomas and Robert, became partners in the London Brewery of Truman, Hanbury and Buxton. Of the two daughters, Elizabeth did not marry but Martha maintained the brewing connection by marrying Joseph Morris, a brewer from Ampthill. This link was further reinforced by the fact that John Izzard Pryor married Joseph Morris's sister Hannah.

It was this generation of the Pryors that severed the long-standing family association with the Quakers as the brothers and sisters at different times in their lives left the sect and became Anglicans. John Izzard Pryor lived in Baldock close to the brewery until 1829 when he bought Clay Hall, a Georgian house and estate of some 500 acres, at Walkern. His three sons by his first marriage, John, Morris and Alfred (in whose names the brewery was purchased) all attended private school at Bury St Edmunds. By 1833, John and Morris were already established in the family business and, with Alfred having now just left school, John Izzard Pryor decided that he too should be trained "as a man of business."

Following negotiations in the City of London, arrangements were made for Alfred to spend up to two years with a Mr Smith in Hamburg, Germany, at a cost of £1,000, to be paid in four instalments. Alfred duly departed for Hamburg in June 1833 on the *William Jolliffe*, his passage costing seven guineas. The diary of Alfred's father records that he received a report from Mr Smith early in 1834 to the effect that his son's conduct was satisfactory although on occasions he was too reserved and silent. Alfred visited his family home in September 1834, returning to Hamburg in October.

At the end of two years in Hamburg, Alfred accepted his host's offer to stay on for a further six months at no extra cost to his father, although this led to a dispute some time later and a further payment had to be made to Mr Smith. It would appear that Alfred remained in Germany for several months more than the suggested extension of six months, since John Izzard Pryor noted on 30 April 1836 that he had received a letter from Alfred in Hamburg urging him to purchase the Hatfield Brewery at the forthcoming sale if it could be bought at a reasonable price. John Izzard Pryor was very keen to see young Alfred settled so he met with his brother Robert and his three sons, John, Morris and Alfred on the morning of the sale, 31 May 1836, for a family discussion on this possible new venture.

He proposed that they should purchase the property jointly if the price was right, with sons John and Morris having a half share and Alfred the remainder. He felt that Alfred was too inexperienced to run the operation alone but, with the benefit of occasional visits and advice from his two older brothers for the first two or three years, he would be able to handle the day-to-day running of the business. His brother Robert agreed to the proposal but the two older sons, particularly Morris, felt that it would put too much onus on them. The lack of real agreement within the family did not give John Pryor (Senior) great confidence to proceed. Nevertheless, at the ensuing sale, with the bidding slow, Pryor was tempted to bid up to £24,300 but dropped out at that figure leaving Mr Spurrell to acquire the property for £24,350, still below the Pryor's stated valuation of £25,000.

The failure of the family to secure the Hatfield Brewery was a source of considerable disappointment, particularly to John Izzard Pryor who remained anxious to see young Alfred in useful employment. He therefore arranged with John and Morris for Alfred to take an active role in the business at Baldock to gain experience for the future. It is questionable as to how dedicated young Alfred was to his new position for, a few months later, an entry in his father's diary relates how, having travelled with his sisters to Oxford, he was unable to return home as he "got into a detestable scrape in London with a diseased female. He is now deservedly suffering in consequence. But hopes to get home by the middle of next week."

Early in 1837, Morris Pryor heard that the Hatfield Brewery was to be sold again. Having discussed the matter with his brother John, he informed his father and suggested that if he still thought it would provide a suitable opportunity for Alfred, he and his brother would be agreeable on the terms previously proposed. It is interesting to note that, on this occasion, the initiative came from those who had previously been less than enthusiastic. Were they motivated by a desire not to have brother Alfred involved in the Baldock business any longer than absolutely necessary?

After visiting the Hatfield Brewery to inspect the premises and the books, arrangements were made for a meeting in London between the two parties on 3 February 1837. John Izzard Pryor was accompanied again by his brother Robert and son John, whilst it is interesting to note that the owner of the brewery, Mr James Spurrell, was represented by his brother-in-law, Mr Watney. Eventually, a purchase price of £31,000 was agreed with a completion date of 25 March. During the remaining seven weeks before the deal was finalised, no effort was spared in giving Alfred the chance to complete his education by allowing him to get experience of going through the whole brewing process several times at the Baldock Brewery and also by arranging for him to visit the public houses owned by the Hatfield Brewery to meet the publicans.

Meanwhile, John Izzard Pryor sorted out the financial arrangements for the purchase with meticulous care, calling upon the assistance of several members of the family. Brother Robert, who had clearly been very closely involved in all the negotiations, made a loan of £10,000 whilst brother-in-law Joseph Morris loaned a further £8,000. These sums were passed on to son Alfred, £15,000 by way of a loan and £3,000 as a gift from his father, and thus, with £2,000 of his own, Alfred had capital of £20,000 to contribute to the business. With brothers John and Morris contributing a further £20,000 between them, the purchase was duly completed on time.

The records show that a price of £34,000 was paid for the business, including stock. Therefore, Alfred had £6,000 working capital with which to embark upon his new venture. So it was that this influential North Herts family expanded its brewing interests to Hatfield and the southern part of the county.

Less than a year later, plans were being made within the family for Alfred's marriage to his cousin Jane, the daughter of his father's youngest brother, Vickris. There were three children from this marriage—two sons and a daughter.

The elder son, Alfred, became a Jesuit while the younger son, Edward, took over and continued the flourishing Hatfield business on Alfred's death in 1876. Edward soon brought his brother-in-law into the business and this led to the formation of the Pryor, Reid & Co. Ltd.

The business expanded substantially during the final quarter of the nineteenth century, firstly by the acquisition of the nearby Park Street Brewery, which was leased to Arthur Sherriff and situated on land which ran uphill from Park Street, alongside the old Arm and Sword Yard and the viaduct toward the present Great Northern pub on the Great North Road.

The Company later took over Bradshaws Newtown Brewery, which had been set up by the Bradshaw brothers, landlords of the White Lion pub, at the rear of the premises close to the modern White Lion Square. During this period, Pryor Reid & Co. spread its wings to other parts of the county, acquiring the brewing interests of Benjamin Young of Hertford and then amalgamating with Glover & Co. of Harpenden. By this time, the Company must have become one of the most important employers in the locality, providing work directly or indirectly for a large number of the residents. Further expansion took place when the Company bought Lattimore's Hope Brewery in Wheathampstead in November 1904, just one month before the death of Edward Pryor.

Two noteworthy events took place in 1908 which in different ways must have caused quite a stir, not only within the brewery but also throughout the whole town. In May of that year (as already described in Chapter 2), a fire broke out on the brewery premises, causing extensive damage and destroying the mineral-water factory.

The brewery offices **Burnt-out offices after the 1908 fire**

Then, some months later, King Edward VII paid an unscheduled visit to the brewery when his car broke down whilst passing through the town. The King strolled into the brewery yard, sat on one of the barrels and watched the workmen until the repairs to his vehicle had been carried out. That evening the enterprising landlord of the Dray Horse placed a barrel on the bar on which was written "King Edward sat here".

Such a scoop could not go unchallenged and by the following night, it is said, that every public house in the town had a barrel on its bar with the identical claim.

All too soon, with the outbreak of the First World War, the established way of life, which had developed in this country during the Victorian age, was totally disrupted, with the inhabitants of Hatfield and the employees of the Brewery all affected by the changes.

Pryor Reid employees

Many of the staff were called to arms and among those destined never to return was the only son of the chairman of the Company, Mr Percy C Reid. There is no doubt that the closure of the brewery in 1920 came about as a direct result of this tragic event since it is recorded that, at the closing dinner for all the employees, held at the One Bell pub, the chairman publicly stated that he would never have thought of closing but for the death of his son. One can but speculate how differently this part of Old Hatfield might have developed had the young Lieutenant Geoffrey Reid survived to fulfil his father's dream of continuing the family business.

Parade at the entrance to the brewery yard

At the time of its closure, the Brewery Company owned approximately one hundred public houses in and around Hatfield and in other parts of the county, all of which were sold to Benskins of Watford. The site of the brewery was acquired by W Waters & Co. who built their garage in a prominent position on the bend at the bottom of Brewery Hill. For those who know that part of Hatfield only in its present layout, I should perhaps explain that the foundations of the brewery now lie buried somewhere beneath the modern precinct known as Salisbury Square.

Chapter 6   **Memories of Hatfield Park**

HATFIELD Park with its vast open green spaces and ancient woodland has had a significant impact on the development of the town over centuries. In former times the Estate was a major employer of labour in the district and the Park continues to be a great asset to local residents, particularly those living in the "Old Town", offering a full programme of concerts, fairs and festivals, charity events and diverse other activities. These events also attract large audiences from far and wide and, whilst in Hatfield, many of the visitors may well be tempted to include a tour of Hatfield House or spend time in the Stable Yard or the Old Palace.

My earliest recollections of the Park go back to the end of the Second World War when we went there as a family to celebrate VE Day—and I believe VJ Day—with bonfire parties. Although these are my earliest recollections of the Park, I understand that my first visit was at the age of three months when I was taken by my mother to a garden party for all the Estate tenants to celebrate the Golden Wedding of the Fourth Marquess and Marchioness of Salisbury.

In the early post-war years there were regular fêtes in the grounds of the House—usually held on Bank Holidays I seem to recall. These fêtes attracted large crowds and gave local residents the chance to see those secret parts of the Park such as the maze and the lake. My lasting memory of these occasions is a fancy-dress competition at one of the fêtes where I went along in a most uncomfortable costume dressed as Mr Therm (the old Gas Board's emblem) and came away jubilant having won third prize, 2s 6d.

> Marquess & Marchioness of Salisbury
> request the pleasure of the company of
> Mr A Lawrence
> at a Garden Party at Hatfield House
> on Saturday, June 19th
> on the occasion of their Golden Wedding.
>
> R.S.V.P.
> The Private Secretary,   4 - 7 p.m.
> Hatfield House.

My mother's invitation to the Garden Party at Hatfield House

The Fourth Marquess and Marchioness of Salisbury
(this photo accompanied the above invitation)

For many years up until the outbreak of the Second World War, one of the regular events to be held annually in the Park was the Hertfordshire Show. The build-up to this highlight of the county calendar would undoubtedly have created great excitement throughout the town. During the inter-war years, there were many other occasions when the Park was the focal point of activity locally. A series of fairs and fêtes held in the 1920s and 1930s were very elaborate events and involved a great deal of organisation by the local community. On Friday 30 and Saturday 31 May 1924, The Hatfield Elizabethan Fête in aid of the Hertfordshire Nursing Association was held in the Park and was attended on the Saturday by Her Royal Highness the Duchess of York (Queen Elizabeth the Queen Mother in later years). It seems slightly odd that the admission charge on the Friday was 5s 0d whereas on the Saturday, when the Royal visitor attended, it was reduced to 1s 6d.

The fête opened with an historical procession with characters dressed as King James I and members of his court, followed by a masque, dramatic performances, a Japanese Play, and Country and Grecian Dancing. A Market Place was erected together with a Village Green, complete with stocks and whipping-post and an old English Fair. In addition, the House and the maze were open to the public and there was boating on the lake.

In Coronation Year (1937) on the August Bank Holiday, "An Elizabethan Pageant & Dickens Fair" was held and created quite a stir. The first episode of the pageant, set in 1588, opened with trumpets heralding the defeat of the Spanish Armada and Good Queen Bess riding through the village bidding her subjects to rejoice. The second episode seemed rather loosely connected with the first in that it depicted a cricket match between Hatfield and The Pickwick Club, complete with Mrs Bardell and Mr Pickwick. An attraction with greater historical accuracy was the tableau of the "Princess in the Tower", recreating the period of Elizabeth I's "partial imprisonment" in the Old Palace at Hatfield prior to her accession to the Throne. The programme included an intriguing variety of sideshows.

Along with more recognisable stalls like darts and hoopla, there were items such as "Strung Leg Mutton", "Kill the Rat", "Bunty Pulls the String", as well as "Stella, the Fortune Teller" and "Mrs Jarley's Waxworks."

Music throughout the day was provided by the Luton Band and the festivities culminated with dancing in the evening on the South Front of Hatfield House.

The event must have proved to be a resounding success as, a year later, a similar format was used for the "Olde Englishe Fayre".

The 1937 programme

The 1937 Pageant

Many of the previous year's attractions were repeated but, this time, Children's Country Dancing, Bicycle Polo and an Ankle Competition were included, with music provided by the St Albans City Prize Silver Band.

It is apparent that, at the time of these Bank Holiday Fairs, people were beginning to realise that Hatfield was experiencing significant developments which would change the face of the town quite dramatically. In his foreword to the programme for both events, the Rector, Pat Leonard, made reference to Hatfield's past and then went on to add, "It also has a future, of that none can doubt, and therein lies the problem." He made reference to the factory development across the "great arterial By-Pass road with its ceaseless hum of hurrying cars and lorries, where once were quiet fields and leafy lanes." He acknowledged the need for additional housing and services and the inevitability of the "mushroom growth", stressing "the crying need for a meeting place where the social life of the new community may find a natural centre". He explained that Lord Salisbury had given a site and that plans had been prepared for the building of a Church Hall and Community Centre to meet this need. He called for the support of all those present at the Fair to bring this plan to fruition. The response must have been very positive as the new Memorial Hall in St Albans Road, dedicated to the memory of a former rector, Lord William Cecil, was opened on 15 October 1938.

Of course, the outbreak of the Second World War brought a halt to most of the organised events in the Park. The House became a military hospital and the Home Guard used the Park for training exercises, but it remained an attractive playground for local children. After a fall of snow, it had special appeal as children of all ages hurried along through the main gates dragging their home-made sledges and headed for the Green Hill or Elephant Dell.

For many years, the Park fulfilled a significant role in the sporting life of Hatfield as, until 1978, it was the home of the town's senior cricket club. Regular home fixtures on Saturdays and Sundays throughout the summer attracted large crowds of locals, as

Hatfield Estate  Cricket Club

CHARITY CRICKET MATCH

In aid of the National Playing Fields Association and the Hatfield Parish Church Fabric Fund

Played at Hatfield Park on Sunday, June 22nd, 1958

Gates Open 12.30 p.m.

LORD SALISBURY'S XI

1. *W. J. Edrich
2. *D. C. S. Compton
3. E. H. Edrich
4. L. Compton
5. J. F. Pretlove
6. *A. R. Gover
7. M. E. L. Melhuish
8. *J. Simms
9. H. Thomson Jones
10. P. Parfitt
11. F. Appleyard

Total

Bowling Analysis

THE LORD'S TAVERNERS

1. A. C. L. Bennett
2. *P. Smith
3. *J. W. Martin
4. R. Smith
5. †B. Barnett
6. D. J. McDonald-Hobley
7. L. H. Phillips
8. W. Franklyn
9. Peter Sellers
10. *J. Young
11. H. T. Bartlett

Total

Bowling Analysis

* England   † Australia

Umpires—W. Whitby & H. W. Shepherd   Scorers—B. Willson & G. Toates

Play begins 2 p.m.   Stumps drawn 6 p.m.

well as intrigued overseas visitors to the House who had never before witnessed this weird and inexplicable game. Visiting teams enjoyed playing in the picturesque setting even if they found it difficult coping with the steep slope down to fine leg and the problem of avoiding passing cars as they fielded on the short boundary alongside the road to the House.

In fact, records show that cricket matches were being played in the Park well over 200 years ago, but two of the most memorable encounters on this well-tended wicket were Charity Matches during the 1950s. The first of these, in aid of the Hatfield Youth Centre Building Fund, took place on Sunday 10 June 1956. Lord Salisbury's star-studded team included Middlesex and England players Bill Edrich (a Hatfield resident around that time), Jack Robertson, John Warr, Fred Titmus (later to become a Hatfield resident) and the charismatic Denis Compton, his brother Leslie and John Murray (subsequently England's wicket-keeper). They were joined by Viscount Kilmuir (Lord Chancellor), Earl de la Warr (Postmaster General) and Lord Balniel, the local MP. The opposition included county cricketers and the television personality Peter Haigh.

Two years later, on 22 June 1958, another Charity Match in aid of the National Playing Fields Association and Hatfield Parish Church Fabric Fund saw Lord Salisbury's XI containing a similarly strong Middlesex contingent face a Lord's Taverners' XI whose numbers included the entertainers McDonald Hobley, William Franklyn and Peter Sellers.

This account illustrates some of the ways in which Hatfield Park has played an important role in providing facilities for the enjoyment of the community during the twentieth century. Other former and present residents of the town will, no doubt, have other recollections and fond memories. Let us hope that whatever development takes place over the coming years, residents and visitors will continue to be able to enjoy the diverse attractions that the Park has to offer.

Goods train passing through Hatfield Station, 1958

Chapter 7   Hatfield's Rail Crash (1946)

HATFIELD shot to the forefront of the national news on 17 October 2000 when, on a sunny autumn Tuesday shortly after noon, an express train from Kings Cross bound for Leeds left the track as it rounded a bend a few hundred yards short of Hatfield Station. We now live in an age of instant communication and within minutes the broadcasters and members of the press were bringing us news and pictures of the horrific scene. The images we saw that afternoon and over the next few days remain clear in our minds, but how much more vivid must they be in the minds of those whose lives were shattered in those few dreadful moments, the distressed passengers and the families of the four men who were killed?

Over the following days, the circumstances which gave rise to the accident were thoroughly investigated and we saw spectacular pictures of the mangled coaches being lifted by giant cranes high above the station and loaded onto lorries to be taken away for detailed scrutiny. A service of prayer was held at Hatfield Parish Church and the line remained closed for weeks causing inconvenience and delays for thousands of travellers, not just locally but those in other parts of the county and beyond. The dramatic events of that October day have been described in great detail in the press and other media but, for many long-standing residents of the town, it must also have made them think back to an accident over half-a-century earlier which had many similar characteristics.

It was the evening of 15 July 1946 and the overnight express to Aberdeen had left Kings Cross on time at 7.05 p.m.

The "V2 Class" locomotive pulling thirteen coaches was in sight of Hatfield Station and estimated to be travelling at 50 mph when, in the words of the driver, "it rolled to the left, then to the right". The first three coaches were derailed with one catching fire. It so happened that the accident took place near the southern end of Hatfield Station, close to the local fire station in Batterdale, so firemen were quickly on hand to extinguish the fire before it caused further damage.

Two local schoolboys, Dick Sherman—whose father was at that time licensee of the Dray Horse public house in old Hatfield—and his friend Bryan Clements happened to be sitting by the line engaged in a popular pastime, collecting train numbers. They provided a vivid description of events, commenting that the train was pretty wobbly as it came round the bend with the tender going one way and the boiler the other. The wobble was like a snake; the tender and first carriages went up, leaving the line. There were clouds of smoke, the coaches turned over and the line was no longer there.

In the case of the derailment in 2000, as soon as the emergency services arrived on the scene, the whole area was sealed off from the public and the professionals took full control with the voluntary organisations in the background, whereas in 1946, members of the public and several voluntary bodies were closely involved in the rescue efforts. It should be remembered that the 1946 crash happened barely a year after the end of the Second World War and people generally were attuned to dealing with disasters. Local doctors were quickly on the scene together with members of the local Red Cross and St John's Ambulance Service. Eleven injured passengers were taken to hospital, the majority going to Hill End Hospital in St Albans where the most serious casualty had to have a leg amputated. A young couple and their baby had arrived in England from South Africa only that morning. The parents were taken to Hill End with slight injuries unaware that their baby had been taken to another hospital at Potters Bar. Thankfully the family was reunited a few hours later.

Meanwhile, back at the scene of the accident, passengers from the crowded train, including many servicemen and holiday-makers, were being cared for by staff from Hatfield Station and local residents, whilst youngsters from a Hatfield Boy Scouts Troop helped to collect up luggage and clothing strewn over the track.

The waiting-room at Hatfield Station became an emergency dressing station and the station buffet served over three hundred cups of tea in the first hour. Fortunately the busy station had a full range of services in those days and was therefore better equipped to provide support than is available in the very basic structure that exists today. The long-since demolished "Royal Waiting Room" was used by the St John's Ambulance Brigade as their headquarters. This was thanks to the initiative shown by a porter who, knowing that a key was not immediately available, used a shovel in order to break in and reach the first-aid equipment.

Amid all the distress and confusion, there were some amusing stories to emerge, such as the party of sailors travelling in the rear coach who, for some inexplicable reason, had with them three monkeys. The sailors tied their monkeys to some luggage at the side of the track while they helped with the rescue work. Meanwhile the schoolboys, who were helping to clear the track, discovered some crates of fruit in the goods van, so were rewarded for their efforts with a few strawberries. The most bizarre item reported to have been found among the wreckage was a coffin which was being taken to Aberdeen for burial.

Local residents made offers of overnight accommodation to some of the passengers but reports indicate that the railway company—in those pre-nationalisation days the LNER—had organised, within an hour-and-a-half, an alternative service from Hatfield to Hitchin from where uninjured passengers could make connections for their journeys north.

Gangs of workmen continued working to clear and repair the tracks and, by the middle of the following morning, the southbound line was back in operation. It is interesting to note that the first train to pass over it was the Royal Train carrying the King, Queen and the two Princesses on their return to London from their holiday at Sandringham. It is said that two hundred workmen "downed tools" to cheer the Royal Party as the train approached at walking pace.

This reflects a dramatic change in public attitudes over the following half-century during which other considerations, such as the possibility of criminal charges and health & safety requirements, gradually assumed prime importance. The derailment on Tuesday 17 October 2000 resulted in the line being out of action for a lengthy period whilst the most thorough investigation was carried out. It also proved to be a watershed for the rail industry in this country, with safety assuming the highest priority over punctuality and growth.

Hatfield's association with the railway goes back over 165 years to 1850 when the Great Northern Railway opened its line from London to Peterborough. In fact, in the golden era of rail travel, Hatfield boasted its own engine sheds and turntable and served as a junction for three branch lines, one running to St Albans Abbey Station (now part of the Alban Way Cycle Route), another to Luton and Dunstable and a third to Hertford. The last two of these lines followed the main line before branching off at a point close to the present Welwyn Garden City Station.

With this amount of activity, there must have been numerous other incidents which attracted less publicity over the years. There is mention of a collision at Hatfield Station leaving seven people seriously injured less than two months after the line opened in 1850, and also of the night "Scotsman" running into a broken-down goods train at Hatfield in 1878. There are spectacular old photographs of an accident on 24 November 1905 at the junction of the mainline and the St Albans Branch line at the northern end of the station showing up-turned goods wagons strewn across the track and smoke belching forth at several points.

In 1964, as a goods train was approaching Hatfield Station, several wagons were derailed and some of the wreckage severely damaged the footbridge which ran from Beaconsfield Road to the

Railway accident at Hatfield, 24 November 1905

Great North Road. One section of the footbridge had to be replaced and I recall that for many years thereafter the two halves were at slightly different levels. There was also the collapse of the Wrestlers Bridge in 1966 (see Chapter 8) when a major road and rail disaster was averted purely by good fortune. No doubt, there are still a number of former railwaymen who were based at Hatfield and formed part of the town's considerable railway population with other interesting amusing or hair-raising tales of their days on the line.

The Wrestlers Bridge, Great North Road, shortly after the collapse

Workmen dismantling the collapsed structure

Chapter 8   Collapse of the Wrestlers Bridge (1966)

IT was a few minutes before 11 a.m. on Sunday 20 February 1966 when I realised that something was wrong. I had been sitting reading the newspaper at home and decided that it was time for a coffee. I went into the kitchen and turned the tap but the flow of water soon became a trickle. I turned on the gas but the supply was not there. From the lounge window it was clear that things were not normal; it was so quiet with the absence of the usual steady stream of traffic. Word soon spread that there was a major problem up at the Wrestlers Bridge. In fact the bridge had collapsed and a busy road had suddenly become a cul-de-sac.

The Wrestlers Bridge had been built in 1850 and, until the A1 was diverted away from Hatfield old town in 1953, it had formed part of the premier trunk road from London to the North East and on to Scotland. Although the road was then reclassified as the A1000, it continued to bear the name of the Great North Road and was still heavily used as it linked with the new A1 only a few hundred yards further north, close to the site of the present Tesco Store by Oldings Corner. Beneath the bridge ran the six tracks of British Rail's East Coast Main Line to York, Newcastle and Edinburgh.

The collapse of the bridge took place at 10.50 a.m. when one of the piers began to crumble and the eastern arch fell onto the line. The last northbound train had passed under the bridge at 10.30 a.m. and the last southbound train went through just a couple of minutes before the dramatic fall. Prompt action by the men working on the track nearby prevented any other trains entering that section of the line but it was little short of a miracle that no traffic was on the road crossing the bridge as the gulf opened up.

The official Ministry of Transport report on the accident revealed that discussions had been taking place since 1960 concerning the abandonment of the road bridge and its replacement by a new bridge for use by pedestrians and cyclists, and to carry telephone, water and gas services, but no firm plans had been drawn up. The bridge had been subject to regular inspections over the years and minor repairs had been undertaken from time to time. In 1965, the Divisional Civil Engineer had recommended that the bridge should be reconstructed by the early part of 1967 unless the proposed closure of the bridge had taken place in the meantime. The bridge was due for its next regular inspection at the time of the collapse.

On Sunday 20 February 1966, a maintenance team was scheduled to re-lay a length of track on the London-bound fast line which ran beneath the bridge. The work, known as blanketing, involved excavating to a depth of almost four feet in order to prepare a new bed for the track. This part of the operation had been completed several hours before the collapse but the subsequent enquiry, not surprisingly, concluded that the excavation work under the bridge had caused the movement of the east pier and resulted in the collapse of the east arch. The report suggests that the preparations for the maintenance work were not as thorough as they should have been and it would seem that the poor state of the bridge was not fully appreciated.

It was largely a matter of good fortune that Hatfield was not the scene of a major disaster on that February Sunday morning. For the local residents, particularly those living to the north of the bridge, it brought about significant changes to their lives. Having been used to living alongside a busy road for years they suddenly found themselves in a relatively quiet backwater. Their water and gas supplies were restored within a few hours and clearance of the debris on the track commenced immediately. By midday on Tuesday, the first of the lines was opened and by 9.00 a.m. on the Wednesday, rail services were almost back to normal with four lines operational. The remaining two lines had trestles erected on them to support the temporary bridge carrying the telephone cables. It was, however, not until some nine months later that the present footbridge was constructed and the lack of this facility was a major inconvenience to many of the local people who had used the old bridge on a daily basis. I well recall the local publican at the Wrestlers pub bemoaning his fate and claiming that he had lost all his passing trade. In fact, the reverse became true because the opportunity was taken to rebuild the old pub and, ever since, it has become a popular hostelry with ample car-parking facilities which could never have existed while the road was in use.

The present-day footbridge which replaced the collapsed road bridge

An aluminium-framed "prefab" erected in Birchwood after WW2

Chapter 9   The Post-War Prefabs

MY earliest memories as a small boy growing up during the Second World War were of evacuees, soldiers and rationing. Even when peace returned in 1945, most things did not change very rapidly, once the street parties and other celebrations connected with VE Day and VJ Day were over.

For me, one of the first changes that I became aware of was the coming of the "prefabs" (prefabricated houses). I was then living in a cottage surrounded by fields which had been cultivated, probably for centuries. The land formed part of Birchwood Farm which was then farmed by the Crawford family. Throughout the war, I had seen the crops grow and knew that, by August, the wheat or oats would have been harvested and those fields would become my playground until the following Spring.

However, in 1946, things began to change. Some of the fields were not ploughed by the teams of horses as they had been in previous years and no crops were sown. Instead, men began staking out the ground. Little did I realise that this activity signalled the loss of my informal playground and was part of a nationwide scheme to tackle one of the most pressing problems of the early post-war years.

Realising that a massive house-building programme would be one of the highest priorities once hostilities ceased, the government launched a Temporary Housing Programme in 1944. It was estimated that almost three-and-a-half million dwellings would be required to provide a home for each family desiring one, taking account of the number of properties destroyed or damaged during the war years, plus a further half-a-million to complete the slum-clearance programme which had been suspended in 1939. A prototype bungalow, commonly called the Portal Bungalow after the Minister, was designed by the Ministry of Works. This was built and put on display at the Tate Gallery in May 1944 and, although the prototype was never put into production, it formed the basis of the programme subsequently embarked upon.

The prototype construction was based on the use of pressed-steel and plywood but before they went into production it was necessary to find alternative materials, which were not in such great demand in other industries. Another consideration was the shortage of skilled labour with experience of the building trade. To overcome this problem, it was decided to employ procedures which would enable the structures to be mass-produced in factories previously engaged in aircraft and armament manufacture, where spare capacity now existed. Although the prototype Portal Bungalow never went into production in its original form, four different types of prefab were developed using a combination of traditional building materials in the most economical way, or other materials not previously associated with housing, e.g. aluminium.

The four revised versions of the bungalow were the Arcon (steel-framed, clad in asbestos cement), the Uni-Seco (timber-framed and asbestos cement panels), the Tarran (reinforced concrete panels and light timber frame) and the Aluminium Bungalow. Within these four types, eleven variations were developed and, between 1946 and 1949, over 150,000 were built.

Of the different types, the Aluminium ones were the most popular, contributing over a third of the total. They were also the most costly with an initial projected cost of £1,365, but this figure escalated over the production period. It is said that, at their peak, they were being produced at the rate of one every twelve minutes and that the four sections supplied by the factory could be erected in thirty to forty man-hours.

From the beginning of 1946, preparations for implementing this massive temporary housing programme were getting underway in towns and villages throughout the country, but my young eyes were firmly fixed on the strange activities taking place in the field on the other side of our garden fence. It quickly became apparent that this was to be the site of Hatfield's first prefabs, 66 concrete-sectional bungalows of the Tarran type in the road that was to become Farm Way (now renamed Drovers Way). In fact, the road had been laid with a concrete base before the war, indicating that it had already been identified as the site for the expansion of the Birchwood Estate when domestic building ceased some six years earlier.

Once the bases had been laid out, the bungalows soon began to take shape in formal rows, each with a sizeable rear garden since, in those days, the tenants would expect to grow most of their own vegetables and some would also wish to keep a few chickens. There would also be a neat front garden, probably with flower beds and a small lawn, as thoughts of a car-owning population with front gardens used as hard-standing for their vehicles were way beyond everyone's comprehension.

The accommodation comprised a living room, with a slow-burning stove and back boiler, with air ducts, to provide warmth to the two bedrooms and hall as well as hot water to the kitchen and bathroom. The specification boasted that the boiler could provide hot bath-water within fifty minutes. The kitchen was well equipped with built-in cupboards and a refrigerator. Tenants were also provided with a garden shed where they stored their fuel and probably the family bicycles.

Once the new dwellings had been allocated by Hatfield Rural District Council, at a rental of 17s 1d per week, to include electricity, water and local rates, the local press reported that a storm had broken out because some of the bungalows were being given to priority candidates with distant addresses and in some cases to childless couples. The local Labour Party sought a suspension pending investigations and the Communist Party sought a public enquiry. However, the Council was supported by the Minister of Health who ruled that it was "working in a fair and reasonable way".

The initial rent may sound a paltry sum in today's terms but, in those days, it must have accounted for a major part of the family budget, bearing in mind that in most families there was only one wage-earner. Certainly it was more than double the amount being paid by my parents to a private landlord.

I recall going into one of the earliest of the bungalows to be occupied since it had been allocated to one of my Primary School teachers who had come into the district from South Wales with her husband. As a boy who lived in a Victorian cottage with only gas lighting, an outdoor lavatory and just cold running water, I was astonished to see all these modern fittings, particularly in the kitchen and bathroom. However, the most memorable feature for me was the "fridge", where my teacher had filled the ice container with water into which she had put some orange juice so I was able to sample an ice lolly—something I had never seen before since an ice cream was the rarest of treats.

As this project was coming to an end, a further development got underway with the building of twenty-four semi-detached, two-storey prefabricated houses with three bedrooms, to meet the needs of larger families, at the western end of Farm Way, near the Hopfields public house. They were officially called "Howard Houses" but became known locally as "the double-deckers" or the "steel houses", presumably because they were early examples of houses with steel frames and partial steel cladding developed from 1944 onwards by the British Iron and Steel Federation.

Children outside their Prefabs

It was not long before the field to the north of Farm Way backing onto the gardens of some of the prefabs became a construction site and new roads appeared. Permission had been given for the erection of a further 105 prefabs on this site. They were very similar to the Tarran bungalows in Farm Way in size, layout and distinctive shallow roofs but, instead of having the pebble-dash external appearance, these had a smoother finish and were, of course, examples of the Aluminium bungalows. Five roads were constructed on this triangular site, with each road shorter than the previous one. The roads became Hillfield, Great Heath, Wood Common, Flaxland and Little Mead, probably names taken from some of the fields which comprised this extensive farm in earlier times. The contract for the layout and development of this project was awarded to a West London firm, Percy Trentham, and it was not long before our new neighbours were moving into their pristine, modern homes decorated in cream and apple green which seem to have been the standard popular colours of the time.

The specification for these bungalows shows that they were 29 feet 11 inches in length by 22 feet 6½ inches wide (approximately 9.1 m x 6.9 m). The central front door led to a living room on the right and a bedroom to the left with another bedroom, bathroom and kitchen facing the rear garden, though presumably the layout varied slightly according to type.

This development completed the programme of "temporary" housing in the Birchwood area of Hatfield by the end of 1948 and reflects the activity that was taking place at numerous other sites within the Hatfield district and

Children outside Prefabs In Farm Way

throughout the country where projects of a similar type were being carried out. The unusual feature of this development was that, within a small area, there were three different designs of prefabricated building providing homes for almost 200 families.

The acute housing shortage during the early post-war years had brought into popular use the word "squatters"—families and individuals who were without a permanent home and who had found accommodation in temporary buildings on unoccupied land.

There were two such squatter sites on the fringes of the Birchwood Estate, one on the northern edge where there were several Nissen huts and another, on the south side, alongside the Wrestlers public house. There, people who were desperate to find somewhere to live, had brought in caravans together with at least two disused railway carriages. The extent of the housing shortage can be assessed by the fact that the Nissen huts continued to be occupied until 1950 and that the last of the caravans was not cleared until 1954. By that time, more traditional building materials had become available, the building of permanent housing was in full swing, and the fields bordering the prefabs had been swallowed up and filled with houses and flats.

When the Temporary Housing Programme was launched and the prototype Portal Bungalow was exhibited in 1944, it was clearly stated that the buildings would have a life of ten to fifteen years. This timetable was re-emphasised when the first tenants took possession of their new homes. In fact, in 1962, Hatfield Council approved a scheme to carry out improvements in the form of insulation-lining work on the bungalows in Farm Way and fitted glass porches to the two-storey dwellings. These improvements served to extend the life of these temporary buildings for some ten years, as it was in the early 1970s that redevelopment and renaming of Farm Way took place.

It was also in 1962 that the Council drew up plans for a further redevelopment which included the site of the five roads containing the Aluminium bungalows, though it was another two years before work began on clearing the first three roads, rehousing the tenants and replacing the bungalows with permanent houses and flats.

The final clearance of the remaining two small roads, Flaxland and Little Mead, was not completed until 1968. It is interesting to note that the redevelopment of this area resulted in the density of the replacement housing being higher than that of twenty years earlier. Society had changed by then; fewer residents wanted long gardens, while increased leisure time and car ownership meant that more time was spent away from the home and, by then, the "60s" were in full "swing".

Prefab at Essendon (occupied as recently as 2006), identical style to the Prefabs in Farm Way (now Drovers Way) – this photo taken Sept. 1998

So it was that the life of the Birchwood prefabs came to an end after some twenty-five years, though in many other places, including some nearby towns and villages, they continued to serve the local community for much longer. Places such as St Albans, Letchworth and Amersham, for example, continued to have tenants living in prefabs well into the twenty-first century and, such was the community spirit among the occupants, they were quite reluctant to give up their prefabs when the time came for redevelopment. Even in our own local district, a small development of eight Tarran prefabs in the village of Essendon survived—of which at least two were still occupied until some ten years ago. These have now been replaced by a half-dozen attractive modern houses which blend in well with the village setting.

Finally, for anyone wishing to indulge in a little nostalgia or keen to get an insight into the early post-war years, I can recommend a visit to the superb Open Air Museum at Chalfont St Giles where one of the Finch Lane, Amersham prefabs, originally designed and manufactured by the Universal Housing Co. Ltd of Rickmansworth, has been sensitively restored.

Chapter 10 Hatfield's Box Factory

THE closure of the Smurfit Corrugated UK Ltd factory in Hatfield at the end of March 1998 brought to an end an association that had existed for over 60 years. The Box Factory, as it was affectionately known by the locals, had provided a lifetime's employment for many local residents and had enjoyed a good relationship with the community in general and those living in the nearby Garden Village in particular.

During the 1930s, three major new industries came to Hatfield occupying new factories on the fringes of the small but expanding town. The first to become established was the de Havilland Aircraft Company soon to be followed by M Cook & Son, cardboard box manufacturers, and finally, just before the outbreak of the Second World War, Jack Olding & Co., dealers in earth-moving and agricultural equipment. All three built impressive new headquarters in the art deco style close to the recently opened Barnet By-Pass.

Of the three firms, M Cook and Son had the longest history having been founded in 1860 by Mrs Matilda Cook who decided to make, rather than purchase, the cardboard boxes for the embroidered pin-cushions she produced in her South London workshop. Over the next half century, the small firm traded from various premises such as Cornwall Road, Lambeth, Great Guildford Street and Sumner Street, Southwark. Early trade directories describe them as Fancy Box Makers but, as their range of activities grew, they were listed as cardboard box makers.

In 1905, Mr H F (Frank) Warbey, a direct descendant of the founder, and said to be her great-great-grandson, became head of

Cooks Corrugated Cases Ltd – the "Box Factory" (since demolished)

The de Havilland Aircraft Company Ltd (now Hatfield Police Station)

Jack Olding & Co. Ltd. The road on the left (the old Great North Road) is now the A414 dual-carriageway as it approaches Oldings Corner. The road in the foreground is now Comet Way (A1001).

the firm and, within ten years, the booming business had relocated to premises in Portpool Lane, Holborn. In 1923, Mr Warbey decided to enter the corrugated container business which involved the introduction of new machinery imported from Germany. Growth continued and this prompted another move of premises to Laycock Street, Islington in 1926. By now, the Company's activities included the manufacture of corrugated paper and board, cardboard boxes and envelopes. The extension of the range of goods produced demanded more modern machinery and this meant more factory space.

So it was that in 1936 the Company purchased a twenty-four acre site on land which had previously formed part of John Lloyd's Astwick Manor Farm on the north-west fringe of Hatfield. The factory opened in 1937 in modern premises surrounded on three sides by farmland and the new housing estate on the other side, features which would scarcely change over the next sixty years. It was not long before the factory, in common with most others in the country, had to adapt its production line to support the war effort. Among the armaments produced by Cooks over the next six years were sixteen million paper cannon shells as well as reserve ninety-gallon fuel tanks for fighter aircraft enabling them to accompany bombers on long-distance raids.

The post-war years heralded a period of rapid expansion for the Company. Ever anxious to keep up with the need to install the most up-to-date plant and machinery, the factory was extended on several occasions during the 1950s and 1960s, making it the town's second largest employer of labour with a workforce in excess of 400. By now, it had become a Company of some significance in the packaging field, supplying containers for many of the major names in the food and drinks industry and to manufacturers of electrical goods. This was the era of the "Cold War" and it is said that Cooks was part of a nationwide scheme of businesses with fleets of vehicles on stand-by to transport politicians and key staff to emergency shelters in the event of a possible nuclear attack.

The firm enjoyed a good reputation for its enlightened staff-relations policy with excellent Sports and Social Club facilities, including a Soccer team playing in the Mid-Herts League, a strong cricket team and a golfing section. The management adopted a progressive policy with the introduction of pension and bonus schemes and annual staff outings in the 1950s, including steamer trips down the Thames to Southend or Clacton. It acknowledged the value of a stable and loyal workforce by awarding a gold watch or carriage clock to all staff on completion of twenty-five-years of service. A "25 Club" was formed, which held regular meetings and arranged an annual dinner for these long-serving employees.

The site attracted at least two visits from the popular BBC Radio programme "Workers' Playtime" at which the workforce was entertained in the works canteen by stars of the day such as Charlie Chester, Ruby Murray, Cyril Fletcher and Val Doonican.

By 1956, the success of the Company under the leadership of its Chairman and Managing Director Mr Frank Warbey, who was now in his mid-seventies, made it the target for a takeover bid. Such an offer was accepted from Mr R G Ivey of Hygrade Corrugated Cases Ltd who, for the next seven years, ran the Hatfield business of Cooks Corrugated Cases in full competition with his other factories at Nelson and Southall. In 1963, there was a further change of ownership when all the Hygrade factories were purchased by the Canadian Group MacMillan Bloedel, under whose control the Hatfield factory continued to flourish.

The major recession of the early 1980s left the industry with significant over-capacity and this led to the merger of the assets of MacMillan Bloedel, the Jefferson Smurfit Group and SCA (Svenska Cellulosa Aktiebolget)—all very well-established paper makers— to form UK Corrugated in 1983. By now, the workforce was being reduced with the introduction of more modern machinery and new production techniques but the Hatfield factory continued to prosper. In fact it claimed to be the UK's second largest producer of corrugated boxes turning out one in every forty containers seen on the supermarket shelves.

On Saturday 20 June 1987, the golden jubilee of the Hatfield factory was celebrated on the site with a Gala Open Day including a programme of entertainment, stalls and sideshows and attractions for visitors of all ages, culminating in a big party at the nearby British Aerospace Staff Club. Staff at all levels could justifiably feel a great sense of pride at the achievements of the Company during the past fifty years. There was every reason to view the future with optimism as the management remained alert to the changing needs of the industry and the new demands of their major customers. Sophisticated modern machinery served to increase output, and a three-shift system was employed to ensure that the plant operated twenty-four hours a day during the week on a reduced workforce. However, it was impossible to foresee the changes that were to take place during the next decade.

Aerial view of the "Box Factory", situated on Great Braitch Lane (off Green Lanes) in Hatfield Garden Village (photo taken 9 March 1964)

In 1990, Smurfit Group increased their share in the Company by buying the interest (24.5%) originally owned by SCA. Some four years later they acquired MacMillan Bloedel's share thereby becoming the sole owner of UK Corrugated. This was at a time when a downturn in the national economy was forcing companies large and small throughout the country to examine their operations and consolidate business wherever appropriate. Market conditions forced Smurfit Corrugated UK to contract and close its Hatfield factory. One part of the operation, the Heavy Duty Section, was relocated in the Company's factory at Peterborough but for the majority of the workforce of almost 200, the closure meant redundancy. To mark the occasion, a farewell get-together was held at the British Aerospace Club at the end of February 1998. This brought to an end the link that the factory had established with the town and the local community over a period of sixty years. Nothing of the former factory, with its art-deco building and central tower remains as the site was cleared and replaced by a modern housing estate, thus extending the Garden Village northwards.

Customers and friends in Salisbury Square to mark the closure of David Brewster's butcher's shop, 9 Dec. 1998

Chapter 11 Butchers Bow Out

WEDNESDAY 9 December 1998 marked the end of another chapter in the story of Old Hatfield when David Brewster closed the doors of his butcher's shop, one of the very few "traditional high street shops" in that part of Hatfield, for the last time.

Some local residents may recall that, in the early post-war years, this thriving community was able to support six butchers' shops within the space of a few hundred yards. Three of them were located on a short stretch of the Great North Road in the two rows of shops which were built after the closure of the brewery in 1920. As one walked along from the station into the town at the top of the hill (then still known to older residents as Brewery Hill) there was Dewhurst, some six shops further on was Walby's and almost opposite was a branch of Butler's. The same firm had another shop in Fore Street, where they faced direct competition from Steabben's; just round the corner into Park Street was the last of the six, Payton's.

In those days, of course, butchery was almost exclusively a male preserve though many of the shops had a glass-fronted kiosk where the lady cashier would sit. After serving a customer, the butcher would make out a ticket in duplicate which would be handed to the cashier to whom the customer made payment. Large carcasses would be hung at the back of the shop; rabbits, game and poultry might be hanging in the window and the floor would be liberally sprinkled with sawdust.

The shops in Fore Street and Park Street went back several centuries and in fact Butler's shop in Fore Street, complete with its slaughter house and stables at the rear, had been the premises of various butchers since 1773. The stables, of course, had been used for the firm's horses which, in earlier times, undertook the local delivery rounds. At the beginning of the twentieth century, Francis Horne had traded from these premises but the Butler family from St Albans acquired the business shortly before the First World War.

As the town grew, Butler's opened their second shop in new premises in 1926. It remained in their hands for over forty years but was closed when this row of shops was demolished during the redevelopment of the Old Town in the late 1960s. The closure of their Fore Street shop followed soon afterwards. The premises in Fore Street are now a desirable private residence, but traces of its past remain with the butcher's hooks still visible in the canopy roof and the brass plate bearing the name BUTLER on the front door.

Another St Albans butcher, Percy Steabben, had acquired the other butcher's shop in Fore Street approximately a decade before Butler's arrived. The business had previously been in the hands of E W Horsey, who was related to the Walby family by marriage. The shop thrived under the Steabben's name for over a half-a-century but closed in the late 1950s. It then became an antique shop for several years before being acquired by the brewers and incorporated into the Eight Bells public house when it was refurbished.

Fred 'Porky' Payton ran his business in Park Street in rather old-fashioned premises which had been a combined public house and butcher's shop until The Butchers Arms was closed c.1909. Fred Payton worked for the previous owner of the shop, George Nicholls, and took over the business on the death of his widow in 1931. A lifelong Hatfield resident recalls him with affection as being "almost as much round as he stood in height" adding, "if one could get him giggling, it was hilarious to see Fred's tummy oscillating up and down". By the 1950s, Park Street had lost its earlier significance as a shopping street in the town and it was during that decade that the shop closed and was later pulled down.

The other two butchers at that time were well placed on the busy Great North Road where they had the benefit of passing trade. Walby's, destined to become Brewster's some fifty years later, moved there from Park Street in 1935 and a branch of the Dewhurst chain opened a few doors away shortly afterwards. Dewhurst remained in business until the redevelopment in the late 1960s and the premises are now part of the "Taste of India" restaurant.

Walby's butcher's shop, situated on the corner of Park Street and Arm & Sword Yard, *c*.1900

The Walby connection with the butchery trade in Hatfield is a story in its own right. The family history is described in detail in Part 11a of *Hatfield and its People*, published originally by the Hatfield Branch of the W E A in 1964 and republished by Hatfield Local History Society in 2014.

Suffice it to say that members of the Walby family were trading as butchers from premises they rented in Park Street, then known as Duck Lane, as early as the seventeenth century. By 1838, George Walby was leasing a property on the other side of Park Street at the corner of Arm and Sword Yard, known by the locals as "Blood and Gut Alley". Several generations of the family continued the business from that site until Joseph Canham Walby moved a few hundred yards to the "modern" shop which had just been built on the Great North Road in 1935.

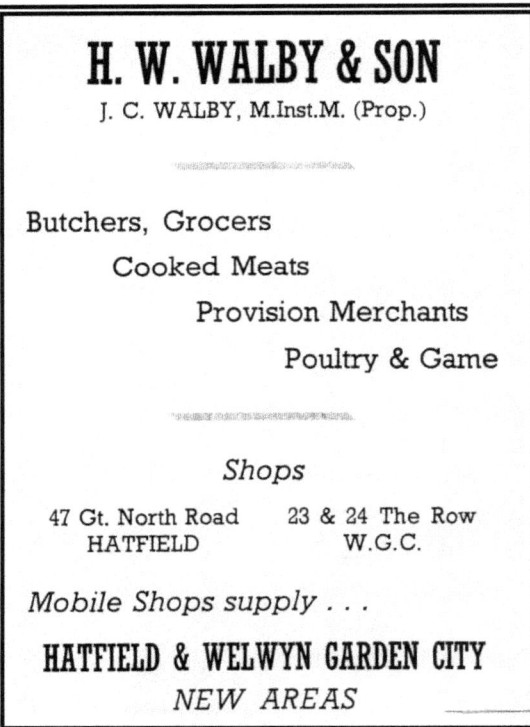

H. W. WALBY & SON
J. C. WALBY, M.Inst.M. (Prop.)

Butchers, Grocers

Cooked Meats

Provision Merchants

Poultry & Game

Shops

47 Gt. North Road   23 & 24 The Row
HATFIELD   W.G.C.

Mobile Shops supply . . .

HATFIELD & WELWYN GARDEN CITY
NEW AREAS

The business enjoyed a high reputation locally and displayed great innovation by being the first in the district to use a mobile self-service shop during the period of rapid growth of the New Town in the early post-war years.

A number of the employees spent most, if not the whole, of their working lives supporting Joe Walby in his thriving business. There was Miss Rumbelow, sister of Sydney Rumbelow who founded the chain of Electrical Goods shops. For many years, she gave loyal service as the bookkeeper and cashier, seated in her kiosk in the corner of the shop. Some Hatfield residents will still remember the cheery George "Razor" Hill, a well-known local character who spent some sixty years working both in the shop and on the local delivery rounds. Finally, there was David Brewster who, with a heavy heart, had to close the door for the last time.

 David had joined the firm forty-one years earlier on leaving school and learned his trade from Joe Walby. When Joe died quite suddenly in 1974, David took over the reins and managed the business before acquiring a fifteen-year lease in 1983. Over the years, he worked hard to adapt to the social changes of the late-twentieth century by expanding his range to include more groceries as well as the traditional meat products. However, with the expiry of the lease, he had to accept the inevitable and, thus, another link with the town's past was broken.

View of Hatfield Old Town taken sometime before 1908 when the brewery offices (still visible here) were destroyed by fire (see photos on page 40)

Chapter 12   Looking Back – A Town That Went West

FOR the benefit of anyone who has known Old Hatfield only in recent decades, I can assure them that, until the 1950s, it was very much a thriving community. During the first half of the twentieth century, its streets were a hive of activity but that was before the planners demolished many of the historic and attractive features as well as other parts desperately in need of modernisation.

For centuries, the majority of the inhabitants of the small town of Hatfield lived in the streets which led down the hill from the three dominant buildings, the Parish Church of St Etheldreda, the late fifteenth-century Old Palace and Hatfield House, and in the streets, alleys and yards which nestled at the bottom of the hill. The remainder of the population would probably have worked and lived on or near one of the outlying estates or farms such as Brocket, Nast Hyde, Panshanger, Birchwood or Roe Green.

During the era of coaching traffic, Hatfield had been an important resting place on the route from London to the north, boasting two major coaching inns as one approached from the south. The first of these was The George which stood on the old North Road at the top of today's Church Street, and which flourished until the end of the eighteenth century. The second was the elegant Salisbury Arms, which still exists as residential accommodation at the top of Fore Street. The arrival of the railway in 1850 brought an end to the coaching traffic but Hatfield then became a busy junction serving three branch lines and with travellers who still sought rest and refreshment in the town.

The One Bell public house at the bottom of Fore Street

The Dray Horse public house facing the Great North Road at the Broadway

Even at the dawn of the twentieth century, the centre of the town supported twelve public houses, the East Indian Chief and the Green Man in Fore Street, the Eight Bells, the Jacobs Well, the Butchers Arms and the Horse and Groom in Park Street, the Bakers Arms and the Travellers Rest in Church Street (or Back Street as it was then known), the Platelayers Arms in Batterdale and the Dray Horse, the One Bell and the Great Northern on the Great North Road.

They varied greatly in terms of size and status but provided suitable outlets to meet the needs of the residents working for the town's main employers of the day—the Estate, the brewery and the railway—and also for travellers heading for other parts. Although the local workers enjoyed precious little leisure time in those days, they must have welcomed the opportunity to spend an hour or two over a pint in the company of their friends and colleagues.

As the years rolled by, many of these establishments were forced to close; the Jacobs Well, the Butchers Arms and the Travellers Rest had ceased trading by the outbreak of the First World War. Two more, the Bakers Arms and the Platelayers Arms, closed their doors for the last time between the two wars and a further four were lost during the 1950s and 1960s: the Green Man, the East Indian Chief, the One Bell and the Dray Horse.

Some of these buildings are now desirable residences and the last two mentioned were victims of the bulldozers during the destruction and redevelopment of the Old Town. Several of the pubs that disappeared would have been very small and only basic alehouses, but the One Bell occupied a prominent site and was equipped with quite substantial function rooms providing good facilities for local clubs and societies. The same applies to one of the establishments to survive the 1960s redevelopment, the Great Northern, which provided similar facilities.

The Great Northern public house (Mr Lane, the proprietor is standing centre-left, in a dark three-piece suit and with his hands in his pockets)

An earlier picture of the Great Northern

The extrovert landlord, Leo Dyke, not only hosted annual dinners for the cricket club and other organisations but was also a regular participant in the after-dinner entertainment that was an essential part of such occasions.

An earlier host at the Great Northern, William Lane, was also a most enterprising landlord who was well ahead of his time as is illustrated in a postcard promoting his services (see overleaf).

I have always found it somewhat surprising that the Great Northern survived demolition in the 1960s as it stands in glorious isolation across from the station. The existence of two other survivors is perhaps easier to explain in that the Eight Bells had been immortalised by Dickens and its popularity had led to its expansion into the former butchers' shop next door, whilst the Horse and Groom was fortunate in that it stood on the side of Park Street that underwent less redevelopment.

An account of Old Hatfield's watering-holes and places for relaxation would not be complete without referring to one or two other buildings along that stretch of the Great North Road. The first of these is the Salisbury Arms built by the third Marquess of Salisbury in 1885 at the southern end of the Broadway, next to the Dray Horse. It served as the town's first Public Hall with a large room on the first floor to accommodate up to four-hundred people. It became a temperance hotel with a coffee tavern on the ground floor and contained a games room for billiards and similar activities for the public. In the post-war era, it became established as a fashionable restaurant with a high reputation for its service and cuisine. Although no longer in public use, the building still stands and its elaborate and distinctive brick chimneys remain a prominent feature on the skyline.

In 1910, Lord Salisbury commissioned the building of a new Public Hall further along the Great North Road just north of the brewery buildings. It was accessed from the main road although the building itself was set back from the road and hidden behind Priory House and another building.

The new Public Hall became the main venue for indoor entertainment with concerts and similar events and served as the town's cinema until the mid-1930s. It was also the location for many fund-raising events during both World Wars.

Finally, mention must be made of the Red Lion near the railway station, which dates back to 1800 and was originally a coaching inn strategically located at the crossroads where the old St Albans to Hertford Road met the Great North Road. Due to its location and size, it has been able to adapt to the changing needs of later generations and has proved that it is still able to attract today's customers with its range of food and drinks to suit the tastes of its twenty-first century clientele.

As in other parts of the country, things had begun to change quite rapidly during the early years of the new Victorian age. The first of these changes, which was to have a marked effect on Hatfield, took place in 1848 when a substantial plot of land adjacent to the Hatfield to St Albans Road, about a mile to the west of the established town, was offered for sale for "speculative development". At the time of the sale, there were just a few dwellings in this outlying part of the district, but no time was lost in getting the development underway. Within a few years, a separate community had grown up in what became known as "Newtown". A handful of substantial properties already stood along this stretch of the St Albans Road but the open spaces between these properties were soon filled with a mixture of more modest dwellings, a few small shops and a number of public houses and beer houses.

One of the more interesting features of those early years was the development of the "Rights of Way". They comprised a series of five narrow lanes which ran north from the St Albans Road on which groups of workmen's cottages were soon built.

The development of Newtown took place in very random fashion and, although the houses were very basic in construction and in respect of the facilities they offered, they lasted for the best part of a hundred years. Within little more than a decade, the population of this new satellite of Hatfield had grown from a few dozen to over five hundred. Some had moved there from the old town while others had come in from outlying hamlets. Despite this, farming remained the main occupation for most of the male residents.

This development virtually coincided with work on the construction of the new railway from London to York which opened in 1850 and had the effect of creating a physical barrier between the existing town and Newtown or as some of the stalwarts of the old town called it, "California", since it was, in their view," way out west".

Another significant effect of the arrival of the railway was the realignment of the main road from London to the north. Until that time, the route from London skirted Hatfield Park and ran immediately between the front of the Old Palace and the Parish Church before turning sharp left down the steep hill of Fore Street—at that time the main commercial area of the town, lined with small shops, coaching inns and beer houses. Now the road would follow the line of the railway, bypassing the Great House, the Church and Fore Street to the east and rejoining the existing route near the long-established brewery and the new railway station.

As the coaching traffic declined and the railway grew, development in the Newtown area continued. During the latter part of the nineteenth century, Hatfield became an important junction for three branch lines to St Albans, Hertford and Luton. The expanding railway population found new homes in the rows of cottages built by the Great Northern Railway to the west of the line, particularly in Newtown. Barriers imposed on one side by the mainline railway and the Park on the other meant that the scope for expansion of the old town was very limited and when the call for more "homes fit for heroes" went up at the end of the Great War, the solution was found by means of further development near the St Albans Road in the Newtown district.

The residential development began near the St Albans Road railway bridge with the building of Cecil Crescent. It then spread westwards along the main road to link up with the new shopping centre. Small shops had existed in Newtown from its early days, one of which had been owned by the Tingey family. The business prospered and when the next generation took over, Tom, the older son, continued with the furniture business whilst his brother John concentrated on the grocery side. In 1919, Tom Tingey, a man with undoubted entrepreneurial flair, built his impressive new Corner House shop on the opposite side of the St Albans Road, which heralded an era of further development for Newtown. A row of new shops sprang up on Tom Tingey's initiative, the largest of which was the grocery store owned by his brother John.

As Newtown grew, changes were also taking place in the old town. The closure of the brewery in 1920 (see Chapter 5) provided the opportunity for more shops to be opened along the Great North Road. These included several businesses previously established in other streets in the Old Town where passing trade had declined over the years. However, the scope for growth was limited and, at the same time, some residents were moving to the new houses on the other side of the railway as their old properties were demolished.

Another highly significant development followed in 1927 with the opening of the Barnet By-Pass which had been cut through the open countryside to the west of Newtown. The de Havilland Aircraft Company relocated on farmland alongside the new By-Pass a few years later and the employment opportunities thus created gave rise to the development of three unconnected new housing estates, the Ellenbrook Estate to the south of the airfield, the Garden Village and the Birchwood Estate both at the northern end of the airfield, one on each side of the new By-Pass. The effect of all this development in the inter-war years was that the town was even more fragmented by 1939.

The first post-war building took place in the Birchwood area on the northern extremity of the town with the appearance of the town's first prefabricated houses and bungalows (see Chapter 9). However, it was the decision in 1948 to designate Hatfield as one of the New Towns to be built in the South East that was to have a profound effect on the town's development and character for the rest of the twentieth century and beyond.

The outline plan for the new "New Town" identified development problems, acknowledging that Hatfield was "an island surrounded by main traffic routes" and "a narrow curving strip between the Barnet By-Pass, main motorway from London to the North, and the undulating oak-studded expanse of Hatfield Park". These remarks hint at the fact that the planners would probably have preferred not to have been directed to this particular location.

Another problem they faced was whether to create a completely new town centre or to build on what they already had. With most of the residential building planned for the southern end of the town, it was considered that to build the new centre in that district would be too remote from the existing town. It was therefore decided to expand the present shopping area along the St Albans Road to make it the commercial heart of the town. Unfortunately, whilst some redevelopment and expansion of this area did take place in the 1950s and 1960s, it failed to grow to the extent envisaged or to attract the range and type of retailers sought by the modern shopper. Furthermore, the ease with which residents could get to the larger and more established centres of St Albans and Welwyn Garden City, either by public transport or increasingly in their own cars, meant that the redeveloped town centre, even with its newly established market, became little more than a larger version of the other satellite shopping parades scattered around the town.

Having completed most of the New Town building, attention switched to the redevelopment of Old Hatfield. A relief road to the south took some of the heavy traffic away from the narrow through-road and many of the old buildings were demolished. Undoubtedly some clearance was necessary but, to my mind, a more selective approach should have been adopted to ensure that this historic part of the town remained a more balanced and vibrant unit than it is today.

I am sure that if this development had happened fifteen or twenty years later, when conservation groups had become more active, the wholesale demolition of this part of Hatfield would not have been accepted. As it was, the redevelopment took too long, some of the trade moved away and we are now left with little more than a ghost town, with just a handful of shops and only a few streets as reminders of the bustling small town of the past.

The arrival of the initially ill-fated Galleria Centre, built over the A1(M) tunnel, which had been carved out in the 1980s to relieve pressure on the former Barnet By-Pass, did nothing to integrate Hatfield's commercial areas, although it has provided residents with a multi-screen cinema to replace the 1930s building which had changed its role to a bingo hall many years earlier.

The Galleria under construction

In the 1990s, two major changes were to have a great influence on Hatfield's future development. The first was the closure of the aircraft factory, a decision which left a huge cloud over the community. For some 60 years, it had been Hatfield's dominant industry and had provided lifelong employment for several generations of local families. At about the same time, the town became the home of the new University of Hertfordshire following its elevation from Polytechnic status. The main building had in fact begun life in 1952 as Hatfield Technical College, thanks to the gift of the site by the then Chairman of the de Havilland Aircraft Company.

The growth of the University during the final decade of the twentieth century was quite dramatic and produced stresses which could not have been envisaged when the college building first appeared on the edge of the post-war New Town residential area. The influx of the expanding student population created pressures in terms of both accommodation and car parking in many parts of the town—problems which are still to be solved.

Former hangar of the de Havilland Comet airliner – now a Fitness Centre

Chapter 13 Looking Forward

AS I look back now, more than twenty years after the closure of the aircraft factory, it is interesting to see how the redevelopment of the site has progressed. Predictably, a new University Campus has been established, with associated facilities including student accommodation. Just to the north of that, a modern housing estate, Salisbury Village, has been built forming an extension to the original Garden Village. This influx of permanent residents and the growth of the student population has resulted in the creation of a new District Centre with retail outlets and supermarket, a hotel and restaurants, a school and a Care Home.

In the early days of the twenty-first century, when a mood of optimism filled the air, there was the prospect of a new major NHS hospital, linked to the University, being built on the site but, before this ever became a major possibility, a change of Government policy meant that these hopes were soon extinguished. Meanwhile, a Business Park began to take shape and many national and international organisations were attracted to the site and set up headquarters and warehousing facilities with easy access to the nearby network of motorways.

Despite all this development, some features from the days of the aircraft works were fortunately preserved, including a pre-war navigation beacon which has been recovered and placed on display. The Comet hangar has been converted into a fitness centre whilst the distinctive Art Deco administration block and the adjacent canteen and restaurant building have been transformed to serve as the town's new Police Station with the original, stylish, gatehouse alongside.

Salisbury Village development building site, April 2003

Art Deco canteen and restaurant block, now Hatfield Police Station

A Heritage Trail has also been set up on the site, providing reminders of the pioneering days of aviation at Hatfield. Bearing in mind the failure of the project to build a major hospital as part of the redevelopment scheme, it is somewhat ironic that one of the most recent structures to appear on the edge of the site, close to Manor Road, is a new private hospital. The western extension of the town that has taken place over the past two decades seems likely to continue as the current "District Plan" indicates that, in order to satisfy the need for additional residential development in the area, more of the open land between the Garden Village and Stanborough will be swallowed up in the coming years.

Former Hatfield Aerodrome beacon now restored on the University campus

The recent transformation of Hatfield's railway station with its new station building, multi-storey car park and bus interchange must rank as one of the most welcome developments in Old Hatfield for many years. Sadly, however, it remains unlikely that many visitors still linger in the historic part of the town for very long unless they are heading for Hatfield House and Park or its associated attractions.

Unfortunately, the surrounding area remains a very quiet backwater despite the much-heralded "Charrette" initiated by Lord Salisbury and led by the urban planner, Andres Duany, now almost ten years ago. That project highlighted the problems created following the redevelopment of the Old Town some fifty years ago and proposed a number of solutions that were designed to inject new life into the district and make it a more attractive location for both residents and visitors.

It goes without saying that such projects are long-term in nature as they have to be undertaken on a phased basis; the development in Arm and Sword Lane to replace the formerly derelict Arm and Sword Yard augurs well for the future but even in these austere times, it must be hoped that the next phase will soon get underway if the original plans are to come to fruition and produce the benefits envisaged. There are examples in other parts of Hatfield where similarly ambitious projects have all too often withered on the vine.

Whilst much development has taken place on the former airfield, it is unfortunate that the much-needed redevelopment of Hatfield Town Centre has proceeded very slowly; it still remains a shadow of what the planners envisaged when they embarked on the creation of the post-war New Town.

An ambitious project was drawn up at the beginning of the twenty-first century but was abandoned when the economic crash struck some ten years ago. This has however provided an opportunity to re-think the likely needs of society in the light of the change in shopping habits that has taken place in the past few years. We are now beginning to see the outline of a revised, phased, programme as the "Hatfield 2030+ Scheme" begins to be rolled out.

We trust that this programme will gain momentum and eventually provide local residents with a Town Centre they can be proud of and that it will fulfil the dreams of earlier generations.

Bibliography

Printed Works

Hertfordshire Countryside, a quarterly (later monthly) magazine published 1946–2012/3. The chapters in this book are based on articles first published in the following editions:

Chapter 1 – Vol. 38, No. 294, October 1983
Chapter 2 – Vol. 50, No. 435, July 1995
Chapter 3 – Vol. 51, No. 450, November 1996
Chapter 4 – Vol. 55, No. 491, March 2000
Chapter 5 – Vol. 41, Nos. 321 & 327, January & July 1986
Chapter 6 – Vol. 56, No. 508, August 2001
Chapter 7 – Vol. 55, No. 500, December 2000
Chapter 8 – Vol. 51, No. 441, February 1996
Chapter 9 – Vol. —, No. 573, January 2007
Chapter 10 – Vol. 53, No. 468, May 1998
Chapter 11 – Vol. 54, No. 477, February 1999
Chapters 12 & 13 – Vol. 59, No. 537, January 2004

Cecil, Lord David, *The Cecils of Hatfield House*, 1973.

Hatfield and its People (Parts 1-12), first published by Hatfield W.E.A., 1959–64, republished by Hatfield Local History Society, 2014.

Herts Advertiser, various editions.

Illustrated London News, 24 and 31 October 1846.

Kirby, Sue and Busby, Richard, *Hatfield, a Pictorial History*, Phillimore & Co. Ltd, 1995.

Pryor, John Izzard, *A Chronicle of Small Beer: The Early Victorian Diaries of a Hertfordshire Brewer*, Phillimore & Co. Ltd, 1970.

Robinson, Janet, *The Tingeys of Hatfield*, Hatfield Local History Society, 2000.

St James' Review, 1907.

Other References

Ordnance Survey map of Hatfield, 1937

Index

Note: Page numbers in *italics* indicate illustrations.

A

A.1 road 57
A1(M) motorway
   tunnel 93
   see also Barnet By-Pass
A.1000 road *see* Great North Road
A.1001 road *see* Comet Way
Alban Way Cycle Route 54
Albert, Prince 21, 23-4
Alexandra, Queen 27-31
Alexandra House 1
Amersham 67, 68
Arm and Sword Lane 98
Arm and Sword Yard 3, 26, 39, 79, 80, 98
Astwick Manor Farm 72

B

Back Street *see* Church Street
Baldock 35, 36, 38
Balfour, J M 19
Balniel, Lord, MP 49
barber shop 7, *9*
Barnet By-Pass 47, 57, 69, 91, 92
   tunnel 93
Batterdale 7, 9, 52, 85
Beaconsfield Road 19
   footbridge 3, *4*, 54-5
Benskins of Watford 42
Bigg, Joseph 35
Birchwood Estate *60*, 63-7, 83, 91
Birchwood Farm 61, 65

Bishop, Ben 7
"Blood and Gut Alley" 80
Box Factory 69-75
Boy Scouts 53
Bradshaws Newton Brewery 39
brewery *see* Hatfield Brewery
Brewery Hill 3, *6*, 7, 33, 42, 77
brewing 33
Brewster, David (butcher) *76*, 77, 79, 81
bridge damage
   Beaconsfield Road 3, *4*, 54-5
   Wrestlers 55, *56*, 57-9, *59*
British Aerospace Staff Club 73, 75
British Rail 57
Broadway *6*, 7, *84*, 87
Brocket 83
bungalows 62-4, 65, 66-8
   Aluminium *60*, 22, 65, 66-7
   Portal 62, 66
   Tarran 62, 63, 65, 68
Burleigh Mead house *ix*, 1
Burvill-Holmes, Dr Leslie 3, *4*
Business Park 95
butcher's 5, *6*, *76*, 77-81
Butchers Arms public house 79, 85
Butler & Son Ltd., T. (butchers) 5, *6*, 77, 78
By-Pass *see* Barnet By-Pass

101

C

café 7
caravans 66
Carter's Pond 16
Cecil, Lord David
   The Cecils of Hatfield House 23-4, 99
Cecil, Lord William, Rector 14, 47
Cecil Crescent 90
Chapman's Yard 17
"Charrette" 98
Chester, Charlie 73
Christian, Captain Tom 11, 15, 16, 17
Church Street (Back Street) iii, 1, 7, *8*, *10*, 11, 83, 85
   fire 13
cinemas 89, 93
Clark, Nobby 5
Clay Hall 36
Clements, Brian 52
coaching inns 83, 89, 90
"Cold War" 72
Comet hangar *94*, 95
Comet Way (A1001) *71*
Communist Party 63
Compton, Denis 48, 49
Compton, Leslie 48, 49
Cook, Matilda 69
Cooks Corrugated Cases Ltd 69-73, *70*
   advertisement *75*
Corner House shop 91
Coronation Year 45
Countess Anne's Primary School iii, 1, *2*, *10*
Cox, Mr (chemist) 5
Crawford family 61

cricket 45, 47-9
cricket club iii, 47-9, 87
Cull, C E *8*

D

Dagmar House *ix*, 1
Daisy Gray's toy shop 7, 9
de Havilland Aircraft Company 69, *70*, 91, 93-4, *94*, 95
   administration block 95
   Comet hangar *94*, 95
   navigation beacon 95, *97*
de la Warr, Earl 49
Dewhurst (butcher's) 5, 77, 79
Dickens, Charles 87
District Centre 95
District Plan 97
Dollimore's greengrocer's 5
Doonican, Val 73
Drage, Dr Lovell 1
Dray Horse public house 7, 52, *84*, 85, 87
Drovers Way *see* Farm Way
Drury Bros. 5
Duany, Andres 98
Duck Lane 80
Dunham, Francis 15
Dyke, Leo 87

E

East Indian Chief public house 85
"Eastcott" *4*
Eaton, Mr (brewery employee) 16
Edrich, W J 48, 49
Edward III, King 35
Edward VII, King 17, 27-31
Eight Bells public house 9, 78, 85, 87

Elizabeth I, Queen 45
Elizabethan Pageant 45, *46*
Ellenbrook Estate 91
Elliott, Mr (shoe repairer) 7
Essendon *67*

F

Farm Way (Drovers Way) 63, 64-5, *65*, 66
fêtes and fairs 43, 45-7, *46*
    Elizabethan Fête 45
Field, Joseph 35
Fielding, Miss (head teacher) iii
fire brigades
    Hatfield 11-14, 15-17, 52
        steam engine 11, *13*, 17
    Hatfield House 12, 16
    Hertford 14
    St Albans 13-14, 16-17
Fire Station 9, 52
fires 11-17
    Hatfield House 11
    rail crash 52
fishmonger 9
Flaxland 65, 67
Flegg (shop assistant) 5
Fletcher, Cyril 73
Fore Street 5, 9, *12*, 26, 33, 83, 90
    butcher's 77, 78
    fire 11-15
    Royal Visit *1846* 19
    Royal Visit *1909* 29, 31
    stables 13-14
Franklyn, William 48, 49

G

Galleria Centre 93, *93*

Garden Village 69, *74*, 75, 91, 95, 97
Gas Board 3
George inn 83
Great Heath road 65
Great North Road 1, 5, 7, *8*, 9, 19, *71*, 77, 79, 85, 87, 90, 91
    A1 57
    Broadway *6*, 7, *84*, 87
    no. 105 (Lawrences' cottage) iii, 1, 64
    Royal Visit *1901 28*, 29
    see also Brewery Hill
Great Northern public house 3, *4*, 39, 85-8, *86*
    advertisement *88*
Great Northern Railway 54, 90
    cottages 90
Green Man public house 85
greengrocer's 5
Gregory family 16, 17

H

Haigh, Peter 49
Hankin, Stan 9
Hankin's
    draper's 9, 17
    tailor's 9
Hatfield and its People 80, 99
Hatfield Brewery *32*, 33-42, 91
Hatfield House
    fire 11
    fire brigade 12, 16
    Marble Hall *20*, 21, 23, 29
    North Front 21, 23, 29
    Royal Visit *1846* 19-24
    Royal Visit *1909* 29-31
    stables *22*, 23, 30

(Hatfield House *cont.*)
    World War II 47
Hatfield Parish Council 15
Hatfield Park 43-9, 92
    cricket 47-9
    fêtes and fairs 43, 45-7, *46*
    on Golden Jubilee 25-6
    Queen Elizabeth's Oak *22*, 23
    Riding School 25-6
    Royal Visit *1846* 21-4
    Royal Visit *1909* 29-31
    trees planted 24, 30
    Vineyard *22*, 23
    World War II 47
Hatfield Rural District Council 63, 66
Hatfield Technical College 94
Hatfield 2030+ Scheme 98
Heritage Trail 97
Hertford 5, 29, 40
    fire brigade 14
    gaol 36
    railway 54, 90
Hertfordshire Countryside 99
Hertfordshire Show 45
Herts Advertiser 26, 99
Herts Battalion of Infantry 29
Herts Yeomanry 19
Hill, George "Razor" 81
Hill & Simmons (baker's) 5
Hillfield road 65
Hollier's Dairy Shop 5
Home Guard 47
Hopfields public house 64
Horne, Francis 78
Hornet, Joe (brewery employee) *34*

Horse and Groom public house 85, 87
horse trough 1
Horsey, E W 78
hospital 95, 97
    St Albans 104
housing 61-8
Hygrade Corrugated Cases Ltd 73

I

Illustrated London News 26, 99
International Stores 5, 9
Ivey, R G 73
Izzard, John 36

J

Jack Olding & Co. Ltd 1, 69, *71*
Jacob's Ladder 7, *8*
Jacob's Well public house 85
Jefferson Smurfit Group 73
Jennings, Mr (store manager) 5
Jessop's (baker's) 17
"Julie's" (hairdresser's) 7

K

Kilmuir, Viscount 49
Kingsbury Brewery 35
Knebworth Hall 30

L

Labour Party 63
Lane, William (pub landlord) *86*, 87, *88*
Lawson's hardware shop 9
Leeke, Mr (brewery employee) *34*
Leonard, Rev. Pat 47

Little Mead 65, 67
Lloyd, John 72
LNER 53
London Brewery 36
London Road 7, 21
London Road School 29

M

M Cook and Son 69
Macmillan Bloedel 73, 74
Manor Road 97
McDonald-Hobley, D J 48, 49
McSweeney's (chemist's) 5
Melbourne, William Lamb, 2nd Viscount
    burial tablet 30
Memorial Hall 47
Mid-Herts Football League 72
Militia Cottages 7, *8*
Morris, Hannah 36
Morris, Joseph 36, 39
Murray, John 49
Murray, Ruby 73

N

Nast Hyde 83
New Place 16
New Town iii, 80, 91-2, 94, 98
Newtown ("California") 31, 89-91
Niccoll, Francis Carter 35
Nicholls, George 79
Nissen huts 66
Northcotts 3
Nott, Mr (tailor) 5

O

Old Palace *22*, 23, 30, 45, 83
Old Town *82*, 83-5, 91

development 85, 86, 89, 90-3, 97-8
Oldings Corner 57, *71*
    Retail Park 1
One Bell public house 7, *28*, 41, *84*, 85
Ordnance Survey map, *1937 2*, 99

P

Panshanger 83
Parish Church *see* St Etheldreda's Church
Park Street 9, 26
    brewery 39
    butcher's 78, 79
    Duck Lane 80
    fire 17
Pateman, J (fireman) 16
Payne, Messrs (saddler's) 11
Payton, Fred (butcher's) 77, 79
Percy Trentham Co. 65
Pettit & Co. (stores) 11-15
Platelayers Arms public house 85
Police Station *70*, 95, *96*
Pond Hill 9
Portal Bungalow 62, 66
Powell, Mervyn (photographer) 5
prefabs *60*, 61-8, *64*, *65*, *67*, 91
    "Howard Houses" 64, 66
Priory House 3, *4*, 87
Priour, Thomas 35
Pryor, Alfred 36-9
Pryor, Edward 39
Pryor, Elizabeth 36
Pryor, Jane 39
Pryor, John 36, 37
Pryor, John Izzard 36, 37-9
    A Chronicle of Small Beer 99

Pryor, Martha 36
Pryor, Morris 36, 37-8
Pryor, Reid & Co.'s Brewery 33, *34*, 35-40, *41*, *42*
   closure 41-2
   Edward VII at 17, 27
   fire 16-17
Pryor, Robert 36, 37, 38-9
Pryor, Thomas 36
Pryor, Vickris 36, 39
Public Halls 3, 87, 88
   Memorial Hall 47
public houses 85-9
   see also names
Puttock's Oak 19

Q

Quakers 35-6
Queen Elizabeth's Oak *22*, 23

R

railway 54, 83, 90
   accidents 51-4
      1905 54, *55*
      1946 51-3
      1964 54-5
      2000 51, 52, 54
   bridge collapse 55, *56*, 57-9. *59*
   Royal Train 54
railway station *50*, 51-2, 53, 54, 97
Red Cross 52
Red Lion Hotel/public house *x*, 1, 35, 89
Reid, Lt Geoffrey 41
Reid, Percy C 41
Richardson, Mrs (wool shop proprietor) 7
Rights of Way 89

roads 90, 91, 92
   Birchwood 65, 66-7
   Rights of Way 89
   see also road names
Robertson, Jack 49
Roe Green 83
Royal Train 54
Rumbelow, Miss 80-1
Rumbelow, Sydney 80-1

S

Salisbury, Lady Emily Mary Hill, 1st Marchioness of 11, 43, 44
Salisbury, Lady Cicely Alice Gore, 4th Marchioness of 27, 29
Salisbury, James Gascoyne-Cecil, 2nd Marquess of 19, 21, 24
Salisbury, Robert Cecil, 3rd Marquess of 87
   statue 27
   tomb 30
Salisbury, James Edward Hubert Gascoyne-Cecil, 4th Marquess of 14, 27, 29, 31, 47, 87
   Golden Wedding 43, 44
Salisbury, Robert Cecil, 5th Marquess of 49, 98
Salisbury Arms 83, 87
Salisbury Hotel 7
Salisbury Square 5, 7, 42, *76*
Salisbury Village 95, *96*
SCA (paper makers) 73, 74
Searanke, Francis Carter 35
Searanke, John (d.*1617*) 33

Searanke, John (d. *1779*) 33-4
Searancke family 33
Sellers, Peter 48, 49
Sherman, Dick 52
Sherriff, Arthur 39
Sherriff's shop and grain store *x*, 3
Smith, Jim (fishmonger) 9
Smurfit Corrugated UK Ltd 69, 74-5
South Herts Yeomanry 21
Spurrell, James 35, 37, 38
squatters 66
St Albans iii, 24, 67, 78, 92
    brewery 35
    fire brigade 13-14, 16-17
    hospital 52
    railway 54
St Albans Road 89, 90-1, 92
St Etheldreda's Church (Parish Church) 1, *6*, 19, 25, 51, 83
    commemorative spire 24
    Edward VII visits 30
St James' Review, The 14-15
St John's Ambulance Brigade 52, 53
stables
    Fore Street 13-14, 78
    Hatfield House *22*, 23, 30
Stanborough 97
Steabben, Percy (butcher) 9, 77, 78
sweet shop 5, 7, *8*

T

Talbot, Rev. W C 26
"Taste of India" restaurant 79
Taylor, Charlie 5
Taylor, Harry (barber) 7, *9*
Temporary Housing Programme 61-5, 66
Tingey, Tom 91
Tingey, John 91
Tingey family 91
Titmus, Fred 49
Topsy's sweet shop 5, 7, *8*
Town Centre 98
toy shop 7, 9
Travellers Rest public house 85

U

UK Corrugated 73-4
University of Hertfordshire 94, 95, *97*

V

Victoria, Princess (daughter of Edward VII) 30
Victoria, Queen
    Golden Jubilee 25-6
    visits Hatfield *18*, 19-24

W

Walby, George 80
Walby, Joseph Canham 5, 80, 81
Walby's (butcher's) 5, 77, 79, *79*, 80
Walkern 36
Warbey, H F (Frank) 69-71, 73
Warr, John 49
Waters & Co. Garage 5, *6*, 7, 42
Watney, James 35, 38
Welham Green Band 31
Wellesley, Lord Charles 19, 21
Wellington, Arthur Wellesley, 1st Duke of 19, 21

Welwyn band 19
Welwyn Garden City 54, 92
Westminster Bank 5, 9
White Lion public house 39
Wildhill village 33
Wilson, Babs 1
Wilson, Mrs (licensee) 1
Winter, Harry 11, 15
Wood Common 65
Woodside village 33
"Workers' Playtime" (BBC) 73
World War I 41, 89
World War II 10, 43, 47, 61, 89
Worrall Brothers 7
Wrestlers Bridge 1
   collapse 55, *56*, 57-9, *59*
Wrestlers Hill 1
Wrestlers public house *vi*, 1, 59

Y

Young, Benjamin 40
York, HRH Elizabeth, Duchess of 45